silk flower arranging

EASY, ELEGANT DISPLAYS

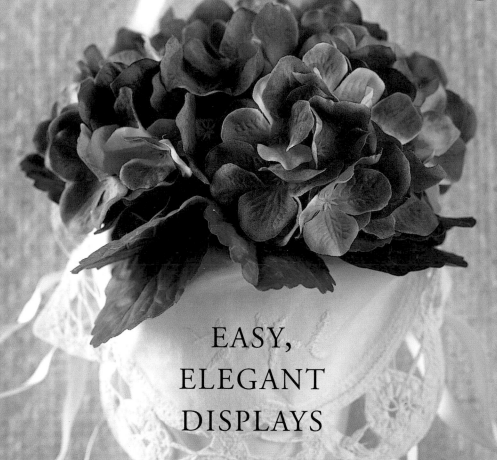

silk flower arranging

EASY,
ELEGANT
DISPLAYS

Marcianne Miller

LARK BOOKS
A Division of Sterling Publishing Company, Inc.
NEW YORK

To
Elizabeth Bennett Cauley
coloratura

art director
Susan McBride

photography
Keith Wright

assistant art director
Hannes Charen

cover design
Barbara Zaretsky

production assistance
Shannon Yokeley

editorial assistance
Delores Gosnell
Rain Newcomb

art intern
Lorelei Buckley

Library of Congress Cataloging-in-Publication Data

Miller, Marcianne.
  Silk flower arranging : easy, elegant displays / Marcianne Miller.--1st ed.
    p. cm.
  Includes index.
  ISBN 1-57990-365-7 (hard)
    1. Silk flower arrangement. I. Title.

  SB449.3.S44 M55 2002
  745.92--dc21
                2002029456

10 9 8 7 6 5 4 3 2 1

First Edition

Published by Lark Books, a division of
Sterling Publishing Co., Inc.
387 Park Avenue South, New York, N.Y. 10016

© 2003, Lark Books

Distributed in Canada by Sterling Publishing,
c/o Canadian Manda Group, One Atlantic Ave., Suite 105
Toronto, Ontario, Canada M6K 3E7

Distributed in the U.K. by:
Guild of Master Craftsman Publications Ltd.
Castle Place
166 High Street
Lewes
East Sussex
England
BN7 1XU
Tel: (+ 44) 1273 477374
Fax: (+ 44) 1273 478606
Email: pubs@thegmcgroup.com
Web: www.gmcpublications.com

Distributed in Australia by Capricorn Link (Australia) Pty Ltd., P.O. Box 704,
Windsor, NSW 2756 Australia

If you have questions or comments about this book, please contact:
Lark Books
67 Broadway
Asheville, NC 28801
(828) 253-0467

Manufactured in China

ISBN 1-57990-365-7

contents

introduction

Real flowers are so essential to beautifying our lives that people have been making copies of them for millennia. Ancient muralists covered the walls of Egyptian pyramids with paintings of flowers, including bowls of flowers on banquet tables—the first record of floral party decorations.

Flowers appeal to our deepest selves. They allow us to cut a snippet of Earth's grandeur and take it indoors. They give voice to emotions we can't find the words for, become gifts that are never forgotten. Our connection with flowers goes beyond seeing them as miracles of nature—in almost all our religious traditions, we use flowers to symbolize aspects of the divine, decorating our houses of worship with their meaningful imagery.

Art history is replete with images of flowers made in wood, glass, porcelain, precious metals, and gems. Artists started making silk flowers in large quantities in 18th-century Paris. A handful of real-silk flower makers remain, their wares available only to those who can afford such luxuries.

The silk flowers that most of us know are actually made of silk-like polyester and other man-made products, such as latex and plastic. Today's artificial silk flowers are affordable, easy to find, allergy-free, user-friendly, and positively gorgeous. Silk flower manufacturers, mostly from Asia, pride themselves on how botanically correct their flowers are, how carefully the petals and foliage are molded, and how lovingly true-to-life they are colored.

Gone are the days when floral arrangers followed rigid design rules that inhibited creativity and terrified beginners. Today if you want the height of your vase to take up more than its previously prescribed one-third of the arrangement, go for it. If you want to mix orange and pink flowers, do it—how will you know if you like it unless you try it? The truth is, for many floral designers today the only rule is "there are no rules."

We hold the middle ground. We feel it's best to know the principles of design first so that when you go against them, you do so consciously. We also believe that you can learn the principles, as well as the mechanics, of silk flower design easily. Contrary to what you may have heard, there is no mystique to silk flower arranging. There's just the magic that comes from doing it.

"Silks," as the professionals call them, aren't mere substitutes for fresh flowers. Silk flowers stand nobly on their own merits, full-fledged decorative items, just as important to a comfortable home as a well-placed pillow or a beautiful lamp. No matter what your décor, and how often (or how infrequently) you are struck by the re-arrange bug, silk flowers will fit your lifestyle.

Art director Susan McBride and I wanted to create a book on silk flower arranging that updated the art for our busy lives, something that would teach us the basics, yet also respect our inherent need to take creative leaps. We wanted designs that were both quick and easy to make, and also sophisticated and elegant—in other words, designs that would impress our friends but wouldn't kill us trying to do so. As working women, we wanted to know how to make stunning silk flower designs without spending a fortune and how to re-use the flowers in new designs forever.

While making *Silk Flower Arranging: Easy, Elegant Displays*, we fell madly in love with silk flowers. We hope you will, too. And may you enjoy reading our book as much as we enjoyed putting it together for you.

7

the basics of arranging silk flowers

silk flowers defined

The term "silk flowers" includes a universe of artificial plants: flowers, foliage, branches, berries, grasses, fruits and vegetables, herbs, succulents and sedums, and anything else the creative silk flower manufacturers will come up with sooner or later. Most "silks" are made of polyester, some of latex and plastic, and a few are real plants that have been dried.

Although we're big fans of flowers that are antiqued, glittered, and dew-kissed, the emphasis in this book is primarily on flowers that look real.

it's all about relationships

Arranging silk flowers is all about relationships: how the flowers relate to one another, to their foliage and other plants, to their accessories and wrappings, to their containers, and how the completed arrangement relates to where it's displayed. Then there is the relationship the flowers have to Mother Nature herself, to the natural environment around them and the changing seasons of the year. Most important is the relationship the flowers have with *you*—how they affect your mood, reflect your personality, and satisfy your creativity.

Just as each element in a recipe is essential for a perfectly baked cake, so do the relationships among silk flowers depend on one another to create an exciting design. You can't talk about flower color without including shape and texture. You can't consider the mood and shape of an arrangement without factoring in where you intend to place it—will it go with the color of the walls and furniture, will it be suitable with the style of the décor and be appropriate with other decorative elements such as paintings or mirrors? In other words, there's more to arranging silk flowers than plopping a bunch of stems into a vase.

On the other hand, arranging silk flowers is not difficult. In fact, after you read this section of the book, you'll realize it's downright easy. The trick is to be aware of the interlocking relationships beforehand so you make the right choices when it comes time to actually buy the flowers and arrange them. This doesn't mean you have to be an expert on all the details. It means you'll want to learn several basic principles and be conscious of applying them to your designs.

It also means being patient with yourself because all artistic endeavors mature by making mistakes. Like the ability to distinguish the scents of different live flowers, your comfort level with the silk flower relationships will blossom (pun intended) in time.

the relationship among flowers

So much emphasis has often been put on the importance of coordinating the flowers with their containers and with the décor, that sometimes we forget that the most basic relationship in silk flower arranging is the one among the flowers themselves. In your designs you want your flowers to have a pleasing variety of color, shape, size, texture, height, and stages of development.

When you make the attempt to put more than one flower into a happy relationship it's kind of like arranging a blind date—the more you think the flowers might have in common, the more their differences come to light.

Do the flowers have five petals, or six, or dozens? Are they tiered like roses or rayed like daisies, spacious or packed, ruffled or relaxed? Are the stamens shy or show-off? Does the flower demurely bow its head on its stem or stand up rigid like a sentinel?

Don't feel overwhelmed. Even as you read the rest of this section and flip through the photos, you'll start to notice the details of the flowers—before you know it, you'll become a flower matchmaker.

9

A realistic way to create variety in an arrangement is to show the different stages of growth of a flower, from bud to partial bloom to full bloom.

the relationship with foliage & other plants

FOLIAGE

Foliage is a flower's distinctive leaves, where the photosynthesis takes place. In your pre-flower arranging days you may have never paid much attention to foliage. But the choices you make about foliage are as important to a good silk flower design as the flowers themselves, which is why we make specific foliage recommendations in most of the projects in this book.

As some flowers have trumpets, tiers of petals, big center disks, or prominent stamens, so foliage varies in its size, shape, texture, and color. There are the sword-like iris leaves, five-pointed ivy leaves, feathery maidenhair fern leaves, and big glossy exotic leaves. Not all foliage is green either: there's the burgundy caladium leaf, the silvery Dusty Miller leaves, and let's not forget the tree leaves that change color in the fall. Don't be shy about moving foliage up or down on a stem, or removing it, in order to create the effect you want.

GRASSES

Though technically different, grasses often get lumped into the foliage category and are frequently used like foliage. Particularly for unfussy environments, arrangements with grass are becoming popular and the silk flower manufacturers are responding with an ever-increasing selection of grasses. Since you might not be familiar with grasses, start decorating with them on a basic level, using them as companions to the flowers, such as the simple grass blades in *Happy Lilies of the Valley* (page 44). Eventually work your way up to using them as the central element in your design.

Long, glossy leaves add elegance to a design.

10

SUCCULENTS & SEDUMS

Succulents and sedums are plants whose fleshy leaves are able to store water for long periods of time. Both are used frequently in live low-water landscaping. In some ways they're halfway between flowers and foliage—they're both greenish in color and they do often produce flowers, even though the blooms are short-lived. You'll be seeing a growing number of succulents and sedums on the silk flower market, so start enjoying them now.

Artificial succulents and sedums are winning over many sophisticated silk flower designers.

An arrangement made with grasses is simply spectacular.

BERRIES, BRANCHES & FRUITS

With the growing importance of Ikebana-influenced designs, branches are being used frequently today, not just as one element in a design, but as the only element. Berries of all shapes and sizes bring a wholly different touch of color to designs and we use them frequently in the book's projects. With their readily identifiable shapes and colors, and the realistic touch they add, fruits (and veggies, too) also make wonderful companions in silk flower arrangements.

Artificial fruits are so attractive, they're worth an entire arrangement for themselves.

Branches add distinctive shapes and colors to designs.

Simple things are the best to wrap flower bunches and decorate vases.

the relationship with accessories & wrappings

The accessories used in silk flower arrangements today are as realistic as the flowers. Most popular are the feathered or wooden birds and glimmering bugs that you attach easily to flowers with a length of floral wire. There are also many choices of dried materials that accentuate a natural look, such as mushrooms, lotus pods, driftwood, and pieces of bark. Other natural accessories include fungus, lichen, pinecones, seashells, and sand dollars.

Ribbon is a favorite companion to silk flowers. Today we use slimmer pieces of ribbon than traditionally, but we also do a lot more things with it than make big bows. In many arrangements, whatever you wrap the flower stems with becomes a major part of the design. Choose it as carefully as you do your other elements.

In addition to ribbon, consider using cord, hemp, raffia, rope, yarn, and even a rhinestone bracelet attached with corsage pins. (See *Daffodil Tree with Gemstones*, page 46, and *Bride's Bouquet*, page 112.) Ribbon can be expensive, so always keep your eye peeled for sales, or buy in bulk and share with a friend.

A clever way to disguise containers is to wrap them in silk foliage.

Realistic insects and butterflies add a special, whimsical touch.

12

the relationship with containers

In most silk flower arrangements the container shares equal billing with the flowers. In the same manner you'd plan a two-piece outfit to wear, so you'd match the container and the flowers in a harmonious set according to style, shape, color, and texture. Do you want romantic and frilly, or opulent and spare, country chic or urban retro? Whichever style you prefer (and remember you can always change it), you want your flowers and vase to work together companionably.

Conventional vases come in a wide range of ever-popular traditional sizes, shapes, colors, and textures.

Colored glass containers offer a double benefit of translucency and color.

Unlike real flowers, which must have a source of water in their containers, silk flower containers don't need to hold water. Thus the range of vessels suitable for silk flowers is limitless—a fact that can be positively overwhelming if you're new to silk flower arranging. Here are some ways to narrow down your selections.

The majority of containers can be classified as translucent or opaque. The translucent containers are those made of glass, crystal, or clear acrylic. The way you arrange the stems in clear containers is an element in your design (see *Calla Lilies in Glass*, page 40). The use of water in the display (or acrylic water; see page 42 for more on that) is also a design decision. If you like the translucency of glass but prefer not to have the flower stems so prominent in your design, consider colored glass (see *Magnolias in Cobalt Blue*, page 60).

Another way to disguise stems in a clear container, and add a pretty decorative element as well, is to use vase fillers (see the two-tone marbles in *Daffodil Tree with Gemstones*, page 46). These fillers are limited only by your imagination. Try glass balls, pebbles, colored sand, seashells, and other things you might not ordinarily think of, such as wool, yarn, or colored tissue paper. With potpourri you gain color and a delightful scent as well.

Opaque containers are those you can't see through: ceramic, pottery, metal, wood, gourds, or any other solid material. Among the most popular opaque containers are baskets, which because of their natural composition always look flower-friendly. Baskets come in endless sizes, colors, and shapes, with or without handles.

Consider the unlimited variety of unconventional containers, such as a hanging letterbox, the bottom half of a globe, your daughter's ballet shoes, your son's forgotten bicycle basket…

Vase fillers can instantaneously alter the personality of a display in a clear vase, and they're fun to collect, too.

Opaque containers hide the mechanics of your silk flower design while helping create its personality.

All flowers have an affinity for baskets.

One of the loveliest ways to express your personal style is by using vintage containers. Many will be family heirlooms. Others will be castoffs you find at tag sales or flea markets. Many bargain hunters will pass up that beautiful china pitcher because it has a crack in the bottom or a chip on the side. You know you can turn it into a priceless vase for silk flowers.

Because they don't need water, silk flowers can be arranged in just about anything.

Vintage containers make treasured vases.

Sometimes the most interesting place to display your silk flower creation is where you'd least expect it.

When you arrange a front-facing shape, be sure to pay attention to the sides too, because they can be seen as you walk toward the display.

16

the relationship with placement

Another key relationship is the one between the arrangement and its location— because once an arrangement is set in place, it becomes a part of everything around it. Know ahead of time where you intend to put your design before starting to compose it. *Slender Inspirations* on page 54, for example, needs to be set in a tall, uncluttered environment. *Mounded Roses*, on page 110, and other low-lying arrangements are ideal for bedside decorations or dining table centerpieces. The expansive *English Cottage Garden* project (page 68) might be appropriate for a company's large reception area, but *Poppies Wrapped in Leaves* (page 50) is more suitable for display in a small office.

Where you decide to place your arrangement affects the shape of your design and how many flowers you'll need. An all-around design is one that is enjoyed from all sides, such as a table centerpiece or a display in front of a mirror. Plan for enough flowers and foliage to fill all sides.

But if you're going to place your arrangement on the top of a bookcase next to a wall, you don't need to decorate its backside. For this front-facing shape, you'd need fewer flowers than if it were the same design in an all-around shape.

The most obvious concern about placement relates to color and the way you can use an arrangement to bring out the colors on a feature you want to highlight, (such as the drapes or pillows, or a nearby painting). You might also choose flower colors that take attention away from something you don't want so noticeable (such as those same drapes or pillows or nearby painting, if you're not fond of them).

Turn the vase as you work on an all-around design so you're always looking directly at the section you're arranging.

four basic styles

For simplicity's sake, we are categorizing the flower arrangements in this book into four basic styles: formal, free-form, linear, and single flower.

The *formal* style is the traditional style of flower arranging. It has a stately, orderly appearance and it's obvious at first glance what geometric shape the arrangement is in. Formal style arrangements usually have a lot of flowers arranged close together, so close in fact, that you often have to look carefully to distinguish them. We tend to think of "cottage" flowers, such as lilacs, peonies, ranunculus, and roses, among others, as traditional flowers.

When you have the chance to acquire multiples of pretty vases, don't hesitate. They're terrific for single flower arrangements.

In the formal style, there are many flowers set closely together.

In the free-form casual style, flowers are arranged loosely.

The *free-form* style is similar to the way kids crayon—sometimes inside the lines and sometimes not. But if you make an imaginary line around the arrangement, you can detect its geometric shape. The most distinctive characteristic of this casual style is that the flowers are loosely placed, so that the individual flowers retain their identity and light shines through them. We present many examples of the free-form style in the book.

Ikebana-influenced designs are linear, spare, and spacious.

The *linear* style is influenced by the ancient Japanese flower arranging tradition called Ikebana. In this style, the lines of the design are prominent. Its composition is spare and spacious, allowing each flower, leaf, or branch to be seen clearly. Often, though certainly not always, flowers considered exotic (those that come from the tropics or look as though they do), such as anthurium, bird of paradise, hibiscus, or orchids are used in this style. It takes many years to become an Ikebana master and understand its rich symbolism, but we have adapted the art's most basic ideas to several projects in the book.

17

Single flower designs are in style now, not only because they are so easy to make, but also because they look sensational. Sometimes a single flower design is indeed a solitary flower in a vase. But more often it's an arrangement based on the principle of repetition: repeated use of one image creates a dramatic impact.

A mounded mass of delicately shaded roses creates a soothing, formal look.

A variety of colors gives single flower designs a cheerful, vibrant mood.

Another way to create a single flower design based on the principle of repetition is to mass together many specimens of the same flower. In general, the more similar in color the massed flowers are, the more formal the appearance of the arrangement. If you use several colors, increasing the variety in the design, it becomes more vibrant.

arranging by the seasons

Once you start decorating with silk flowers, an amazing thing happens. You start noticing real flowers more, especially as they relate to the changing seasons. You take heed of fresh flowers growing in your neighborhood gardens, in the freeway landscaping on the way to work, and in the flower section of the supermarket. Almost every magazine you read, particularly if it relates to home decorating, will have articles on seasonal flowers. So although you don't have to decorate with silk flowers by the changing seasons, doing so seems natural.

It's easy to decorate according to the time of year because silk flowers (like almost everything else) are merchandised by season. Updating your silk flowers every three months is also a great way to avoid being bored by your arrangements. Keep the basic flowers—roses, let's say—and vary the companion flowers.

Because we're used to seeing fresh greenhouse-grown flowers year-round in florist shops, certain silk flowers are used in arrangements any time of year and no one seems to think they are off-season. Other flowers are considered so typical of one season that they seem out of place at other times.

Some flowers, such as oriental lilies, carnations, and roses, are considered all-year flowers.

buying silk flowers

If you're new to silk flower arranging, we recommend at first buying your flowers in craft or floral supply stores—there's nothing quite like actually holding a silk flower in your hand as you imagine its future. Later on, after you've gained experience, investigate buying from mail order catalogs or on the Internet. Type in "silk flowers" on your search engine and you'll find more silk flower sites than you ever dreamed of.

In general, buy the highest quality flowers you can afford because you'll be happier with them in the long run. Don't mix flowers of different quality in the same design—the difference between the flowers is obvious and can ruin the look of the arrangement.

The first thing you'll notice is how much the silks look like real flowers. See how the petal shapes are clearly defined and colored realistically, how buds and partially opened blossoms "grow" on the stem together as they do in real life, and how true-to-life the foliage is (even to including thorns where appropriate). Most flowers have accurately designed stamen—some even have "pollen" on them. Turn the flower over and observe the underside. The mark of a top-notch flower is how accurate it looks underneath the petals.

Flowers come in single stems, or in "bushes" that contain multiple stems of flowers, often of different sizes, attached to a big stem at the bottom. When you have the choice, buying a bush of flowers is economical since you pay less per flower on a bush than on a single stem. In our project instructions, we often indicate to buy a bush of flowers and then cut the individual stems from it.

Realistic detailing is the mark of a good silk flower.

Buying flowers and foliage in "bushes" is economical.

Some flowers epitomize the season in which they grow naturally: spring tulips, summer sunflowers, autumn chrysanthemums, and winter holly with berries.

There are two types of stems. Hand-wrapped stems (usually single stems) are wired and then hand-wrapped with tape; they're pricier because of the labor costs. Other stems are made of plastic, polyester, or latex, with or without wire in the center.

The most meticulous flower arrangers take their containers along to the store to see how they work together before making a purchase. It also helps if you have a swatch of fabric or paint chips so you can coordinate your room's colors with the flower colors. If you buy your flowers on a whim and make a mistake, don't fret too much—you can always bring the flowers back to the store if you keep your receipts. We've put together a checklist of questions to ask yourself before purchasing your flowers. It's on page 122 in the back of the book.

Many of us were introduced to the fun of decorating with silk flowers by buying ready-made arrangements. Although these arrangements can be somewhat pricey, they're often beautifully put together and certainly a good way to instantaneously brighten up your home. Also, taking apart a well-made arrangement to see in detail how it's constructed is one way to gain a terrific hands-on lesson in arranging silk flowers.

The best bargains in ready-made arrangements are garlands, which come in a variety of lengths, and an ever-increasing number of flower combinations.

Try to shop in the daytime so you can actually take the flowers outside, away from the store's fluorescent lighting, and see what your flowers look like in daylight. Bundle your flowers and foliage together in a bouquet to determine how their sizes, shapes, textures, and colors look together. If you like the combination, go for it. If it looks awful, then follow the professional designer's number one doctrine: Start over.

20

Don't use hand-wrapped stems in displays with water because the tape will unravel. It's okay to put latex, plastic, or polyester stems in water.

Carefully study the details of your flowers before making a purchase.

Ready-made garlands are wonderful for last-minute decorating.

tools & materials

With silk flower arranging, you spend most of your money, not on equipment and materials you'll never see, but on the flowers and containers that are noticed by everyone. That's a pretty good rate of return on your home decorating dollars.

You probably already have most of the tools you'll need, or you can find them easily in your local craft or floral supply store.

You need only a handful of tools and materials to cut, lengthen, wrap, or glue silk flowers and foliage: simple cutting tools, tweezers, floral wire, floral tape, and the ever-useful hot-glue gun.

FLORAL FOAM

Floral foam is the hidden heroine of any floral design that needs support not offered by the mouth of the vase. Foam for fresh flowers is porous in order to hold water. Foam made specifically for silk and dried flowers is dry, and very firm and solid. It comes in a regular version and in deluxe versions, which are firm enough to hold heavy stems, but soft enough for smaller stems, too. If, like many people these days, you want to combine fresh and silk flowers, use the porous foam made for fresh flowers and keep it wet.

The packages of foam are clearly marked for fresh or silk stems. Depending on the manufacturer, the colors vary, from different shades of green, to tan or grey shades. They often come in

"bricks" (the size of a brick) with several to a bag, as well as lots of shapes for use with wreaths and topiary. As usual, if you buy in bulk you can save a few pennies.

It's not a good idea to re-use floral foam. Once you've stuck enough holes in the foam to make an arrangement, it's not serviceable for another go-around. The foam is inexpensive enough that you can start fresh for each arrangement.

Tools and supplies that help you attach silk plants are affordable and easy to find: floral foam, serrated knives, and awls; U-pins and moss; adhesive clay; and wreath and topiary bases.

It's floral foam that gives this charming May Basket its firm shape and support for the flowers.

For vertical arrangements, cut the foam to fit snugly into the container below the rim.

Add moss and secure it with U-pins so it covers the foam completely.

For designs that have cascading flowers and foliage, shape the foam above the rim. This creates slightly different levels in which to insert the plants.

If you've never worked with floral foam before, be assured it takes only a short while to become friendly with it. Think of the foam as a stale loaf of Italian bread and you'll know what to do. You'll understand that a serrated knife is the best knife to cut through foam (that's why we always recommend it in our instructions). You'll also know to expect a lot of "crumbs"—so cut your foam on sheets of spread-out newspaper, and then funnel the newspaper and empty the residue into the wastebasket.

Hold the foam firmly on your cutting surface with one hand and cut it with the other. Always cut the foam to fit into your container as snugly as possible. If you need to shape the foam to fit a particular container, then shave it away from your fingers. Use a smaller serrated knife, if needed. Wash your hands after you work with the foam and don't rub your eyes—the foam can be irritating.

If your arrangement is top heavy with flowers you'll want extra security to keep the foam in place. There is a very sticky green tape specially made for working with foam. Use it to bind several bricks of foam together, to increase the height of the foam inside the container. (Use a dab of hot glue on the bottom of the foam to secure it inside the container.)

The tape can make a sturdy grid across the opening of the container that can help hold flowers in place. Cut the foam to 1 inch (2.5 cm) above the container opening and cross the tape in an "X" above it. Leave 1 inch (2.5 cm) of tape on the ends to secure them to the sides

below the rim. For heavier arrangements, tape completely around the container about ½ inch (1.3 cm) below the rim. Overlap the tape several inches to create a strong hold. Avoid piercing the tape when you insert your stems, and cover the mechanics with the materials that will cascade over the vase edge.

Adhesive clay, specially made for floral arrangements, comes in handy when you need extra security in arrangements using flower frogs. Use clay to secure the frog into the bottom of a container. You can also break off short pieces of clay and use them to make wedges to press foam against uneven surfaces, such as the insides of baskets.

In arrangements with many tall flowers, take extra steps to secure them.

Mosses come in different colors and degrees of dryness. Left to right: green sheet moss, grey Spanish moss and reindeer moss

In general, push stems about two-thirds of the way into the foam. If you're using thick branches or stems, first make a hole in the foam with an awl (or other sharp-pointed object) and then insert the branch.

Another trick is to dip the ends of thick branches into hot glue before inserting them, which will really help hold them in place.

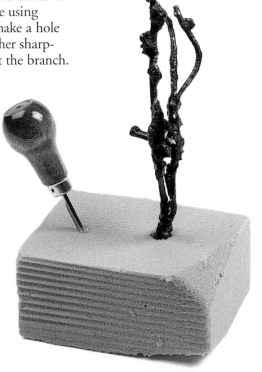

MOSSES

Mosses are the most frequently used "groundcovers" for silk flower arrangements. The most popular mosses are sheet moss (sold in sheets like mini-sod) and several kinds sold in bags, such as Spanish moss, sphagnum moss, and reindeer moss (actually a lichen that's been treated to remain soft and is dyed in a variety of colors). Excelsior, made of fine, curled wood shavings, is a good and colorful moss substitute. Buy moss in quantity when you can because you always end up using more than you think you will.

The purpose of moss is to hide the floral foam, which does indeed look unattractive under your beautiful flowers. The kind of moss you choose is up to you and what works with your design. Since sheet moss lies flat, use it when you want a manicured green, flat look, like moss in a moist forest. The other mosses are dry and look best when you fluff them up. Use a gentle touch with moss—you want it to effectively cover the foam, but not be obtrusive.

In addition to hiding the floral foam, moss can also be used as a design accent.

U-PINS & HOT GLUE

There are two basic ways to attach the moss to the foam and it's your preference which method you use. Inserting U-pins through moss and into foam is not unlike using hairpins. The U-shaped pins are sometimes called greening pins, fern pins, or moss pins.

A hot-glue gun and glue sticks are as important to silk flower arranging as they are to so many other home arts–you can't imagine working without them. There are glue sticks made especially for working with silk flowers which dry more slowly than regular glue sticks, giving you plenty of time to re-position flowers if you need to. Another handy tool is a hot-glue pot into which you can dip the flowers to get a quick dab of glue without having to use your other hand for the glue gun. This is really useful when making wreaths and swags in which you are using many short-stemmed pieces.

FLORAL WIRE & FLORAL TAPE

Reflecting its main purpose, floral tape is often referred to as "stem wrap" tape. The secret to using it effectively is to pull the crepe-like tape taut as you work with it. Doing so makes it sticky so when you wrap it, it will adhere to itself and hold firm. If you wrap the tape loosely it will fall off. Floral tape comes in green, moss green, brown, and white. Use whatever color is appropriate.

Start at the top of the stem and work your way down. Hold the tape firmly on the stem with the thumb and fingers on one hand, and wrap with the other. (You'll get the hang of it quickly, don't despair.) If there's an obvious color difference between the stem and the tape, then go ahead and wrap the whole stem. Leave at least 2 inches (5 cm) at the bottom unwrapped to stick into the floral foam.

Floral wire comes pre-cut in packages with different gauges and colors. It's also available on spools, making it easier to use for projects that call for a lot of wire. Use light gauge wire (such as 21 gauge) to join slender stems and attach flowers and foliage to wreaths and swags. Use heavier gauge wire (such as 18 gauge) to extend the length of heavier stems and strengthen weak stems.

Two kinds of wire cutters should be sufficient, a heavy one for the thick stems, and a light one for thinner stems. A pair of scissors can also serve to cut the thinner stems. To trim frayed flower petals, use tiny sewing shears.

You need just a few things to do most of the wrapping and attaching in silk flower designs: floral tape, floral wire, corsage pins, and U-pins.

You can be certain that floral wire created some of the effects in this arrangement with many flowers.

One of the most wonderful things about silk flowers is their ability to revive themselves. If you accidentally cut a flower from its stem, glue it back on. Do you need extra foliage for an arrangement? Take it from some stems you already cut. Let's say (voice of experience here) you mistakenly cut your dahlia stems to 4 inches (10.2 cm) and now you need them to be 6 inches (15.2 cm) tall. You're in luck because it's quick and easy to make silk flower stems longer. See the information that follows.

HOW TO EXTEND STEMS

There are three ways of extending a stem: use a floral pick, add another length of stem, or just add wire and tape.

Method 1
Floral picks are small pieces of wood, pointy at the bottom, with wire attached to the other end. Hold the pick half of its length against the bottom of the stem you wish to lengthen. Wrap the wire attached to the pick around the stem and then wrap the duo with floral tape. This method provides a sturdy extension.

Method 2
Place a length of floral wire against the stem and wrap both of them with tape.

Method 3
Push foliage onto a new length of wire, glue it in place, and wrap the wire with tape.

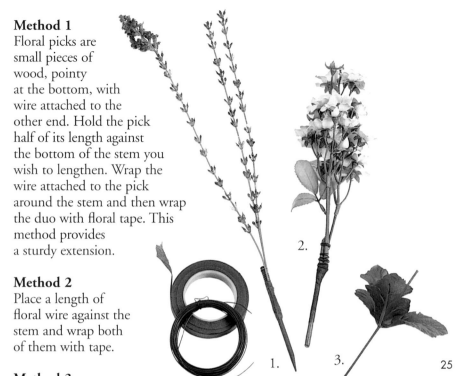

25

FLOWER FROGS

Flower frogs (or floral pin holders) are bases with spikes that hold stems and branches when you don't use floral foam. Frogs come in a variety of shapes and sizes, from as small as a votive candle (see *Rock Simplicity* on page 86) to giant size for professional arrangements. You can find them in craft and floral supply stores.

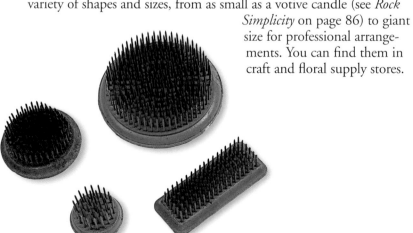

WREATH & TOPIARY BASES

There are as many ways to design wreaths as there are flowers to make them with. The two most common natural wreath bases, and the ones you can usually find in stores, are grapevine wreaths and straw wreaths. Artificial bases are made of polystyrene, floral foam and other synthetic materials, and are also found at craft and floral supply stores.

Topiary is the ancient art of training and trimming plants into shapes. It's making a big comeback in live landscaping and it's fun and easy to make topiaries with silk flowers and foliage. You can buy pre-made topiaries (such as we did for the *Tabletop Topiary* project, page 108) already covered in moss, as well as uncovered polystyrene and wire forms.

Wreath bases are made of natural
ingredients as well as
synthetic materials.

Once you learn how to make a simple wreath,
a more elaborate one is not more difficult—
it merely takes longer.

You can make topiary sculptures
with pre-made forms or make
your own with wire shapes, moss,
and hot glue.

Crown wreaths are wonderful projects to use small flowers and foliage left over from another design.

making the most of your silk flower dollars

Considering how much beauty they bring into our lives and how long they last, silk flowers are a genuine bargain. Even so, in a world that is too throwaway already, it's good to know that silk flowers are the quintessentially recyclable artist's medium. Here are some tips on how to endlessly stretch your silk flower dollars.

• **Get a buy-in-bulk buddy**. Buying in bulk saves you money only if you can use everything you buy. Go shopping with a friend so you can split the expenses and cut down any waste.

• **Remember the Three R's of home silk flower design: Refresh, Recycle, and Re-design.** What this means is learn what flowers you can substitute for others, so you can refresh your designs as the mood strikes you. Never throw away a good silk flower. Save it for a rainy day, to recycle into a new arrangement. Silk flowers don't fade, wither, or drop petals all over the carpet, which means you can constantly re-design arrangements.

27

Stretch your silk flower dollars by interchanging flowers. This arrangement would look equally stunning if you substituted the chrysanthemums with dahlias, lisanthiums, peonies, or sunflowers.

Good storage of your silk flowers and supplies is whatever organizing system works best for you.

Use a hair dryer on the low setting or a feather duster to clean silk flowers, especially those with hand-wrapped stems.

• To be able to follow the Three R's it helps if you always think of **interchangeability** when you buy your flowers and plan your designs. To that end, in almost all the projects in this book, we have given tips on what other flowers, and/or containers to consider if you want to re-design the projects to your own style.

• **Create a good storage system** that allows you enough space to store your silks safely and find them easily. If you have to pull boxes stuffed with old silk flowers out from underneath the bed every time you want to refresh an arrangement, guess what? You won't do it. Keep all your tools, yes, even extra pairs of scissors and wire cutters, along with all your ribbons and other wrappings, in a place that is "hands off" to everyone else in the family—so you can find things when you need them. In our busy lives, every moment we have to work with our silk flowers is precious so we have to use those moments efficiently.

28

Most of the new silk flowers can be cleaned safely with water.

• As you do with other things that you cherish, **take care of your silk flowers.** Keep them out of direct sunlight, which can cause them to fade over time. Dust and clean them regularly so they express their full beauty all the time. In addition to using feather dusters or water, look in your floral supply stores for spray cleaners that work like magic to clean and renew silk flowers.

design basics

Now that we've gotten all the practical stuff out of the way, let's jump in to the part that is the most fun, but is also the most daunting for beginners—the choice of the flowers and foliage and how you actually arrange them. There are five key elements that play a role in making easy, elegant displays: shape, texture, scale, balance, and color. As in everything else with flower arranging, each element is interrelated with the other elements.

SHAPE

In general, flower arrangements follow geometric shapes. In the old days, all kinds of shapes were used, including the grand L-shape and the curving S-shape. If you're interested in these shapes, there are many books that explain them. We prefer arrangements that are simple, suitable to our busy lifestyles, and in sync with our attempts to de-clutter and create more space. Thus most of our designers instinctively used only a few geometric shapes.

Round

Half circle

Fan

Horizontal

29

Half oval

Triangle

Rectangle

Combination of Inverted
Triangle & Drooping Fan

Adding texture to a monochromatic arrangement is the mark of a sophisticated design.

Texture is first found within the flower itself.

TEXTURE

Texture is what something feels like. Is it smooth like a glazed vase or rough like a woven basket? Is it fluffy moss, or hard copper? A ruffled dahlia, or a spiky lilac or a furry pussy willow?

Showing a variety of textures is a mark of sophistication in a design. Let's look at a design that doesn't have a lot of color, such as the *Rock Simplicity* project to the left (and on page 86). Notice the many textures; the hardness of the rock, the roughness of the sand below it, the stiffness of the horsetails and the airiness of the grasses.

Flip quickly through the book to notice how each project has several textures among the flowers, foliage, and the container. What's not shown is how the environment of the arrangement also carries texture—the stucco wall, the rough-hewn table, the smooth marble countertop, the mirror, the brick patio, and the thick carpet. That's because for the purpose of the book, we wanted to emphasize the principles of design of the arrangements themselves, without the distraction of a background. But in planning your designs, you'll want to factor in the texture (as well as the color, of course) of the surface against which your arrangement will be displayed.

Even the simplest display shows a variety of textures.

SCALE

Scale is the height, length, and width of the flower arrangement in proportion to the container. The old design rules dictated that the vase and the flowers had to be in equal 50/50 proportion. Or, according to another school of thought, the proportion should be one-third vase/two-thirds flowers. There's nothing wrong with following these rules when you're first starting out; in fact, many of our arrangements follow the traditional proportion rules.

But we also broke those rules. In the *Slender Inspiration* project to the left (and on page 54), the container takes up only about one-eighth of the height of the entire arrangement, but it works perfectly because space itself is a key design element.

Use the proportion rules to guide you in the beginning when you are working with more traditional designs. Then when you have gained experience, try the newer, Ikebana-inspired designs, which use fewer flowers, and containers in non-traditional proportions.

Scale is also an important consideration in the relationship between the flowers and where they are displayed. What looks good on a pedestal in the foyer may not seem right if you move it to the coffee table. Think of the flowers as a painting and the area surrounding them as their frame—they should work together.

31

Ikebana-influenced designs have changed
the old rules of scale.

This magnolia arrangement
follows the traditional rule of
50-50 proportion between
flowers and vase. Also notice
how many different textures it
displays among petals,
stamen, leaves, and glass.

Balance occurs when flowers of different visual "weight" are evenly distributed

COLOR

Color–ah, this is the fun part, the one that probably attracted you to silk flowers in the first place, because color is what appeals most to the child in each of us. Though you may have studied a color chart in elementary school science class, isn't it still thrilling every time you see one? When you first start shopping for silk flowers, take the chart with you and use it until it becomes part of your intuitive design sense.

Beyond choosing to use flowers in the colors you like, you'll want to creatively combine colors in relationship with one another and in relationship with their foliage, their containers, and their surroundings. Common wisdom tells you that you're always safe with neutral colors, so flowers in the creamy tones make good choices for beginner's experiments.

You can't go wrong with peonies in neutral or delicate shades.

32

BALANCE

Balance is the even distribution of elements that give visual "weight" to a design. In addition to the geometric shapes of arrangements, floral designs can also be considered symmetrical or asymmetrical—a corollary of formal or free-form styles.

Flowers with a symmetrical shape are spaced evenly throughout, making a design that is calm and soothing to look at. The asymmetrical look is more dynamic, with an element of risk. The flowers themselves aren't spaced uniformly throughout the design, but their visual weight (combination of color and size) is evenly distributed.

To gain balance, many designers put the largest and darkest flowers near the base of the design and the lighter elements at the outer edges. But again, these rules are often broken today in favor of achieving balance by other means, such as a variety of textures or the use of empty space.

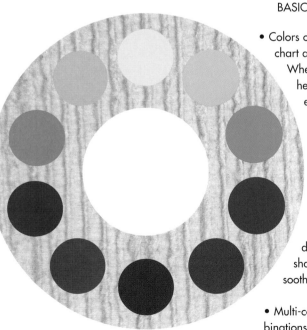

BASIC COLOR WHEEL

• Colors on the opposite side of the chart are complementary colors. When combined, each color heightens the other, creating an energetic effect.

• Colors that are neighbors on the chart, or analogous, create a balanced effect.

• Monochromatic arrangements use the same color in different hues, tints, and shades, creating a soothing effect.

• Multi-colored or polychromatic combinations are lively and cheerful. They attain unity by careful attention to texture and shape.

• Green is nature's neutralizer, bringing harmony to flowers of different colors, shapes, and textures.

You can be safe—and harmonious, too—if you follow another design principle: use flowers that are the same color throughout the design (*monochromatic*) or use colors that are neighbors on the color chart (*analogous*). For example red, red-orange, and orange are good arrangement companions, especially if you separate them a bit with white or pale flowers and greenery.

Energizing color combinations are those with colors from the opposite sides of the color chart, or *complementary* colors. For example, violet and yellow is a popular combination—both colors are made more vivid by being paired.

After you have experimented with many color combinations you'll learn that almost all color combinations will work beautifully as long as you balance their visual weight and combine them with a variety of different textures, shapes, and sizes.

After you've done several "color-safe" arrangements, take risks and be more bold with color combinations.

Greenery harmonizes the combination of complementary or contrasting colors.

the art of combining flowers

You've graduated from the single-flower or monochromatic designs and now you want to try what the "big" silk flower designers do—put together a variety of flowers in different sizes, shapes, and colors with foliage and other elements. You want a display that makes you shout "wow"!

If you've gotten this far in the book (and kept flipping back and forth through it as we referred you to the projects), you already have a good feel for most of the design principles that underline silk flower arranging. Now your goal is to apply those principles to a variety of specific flowers.

Rather than becoming overwhelmed by the prospect of doing it all, break down a multi-flower arrangement into manageable elements—then it becomes easy.

Many designers simply divide flowers and foliage into three basic categories, based usually on height and size. The categories are meant as a helpful guide, but don't feel you have to follow them slavishly.

It's amazing how many colors, sizes, shapes, and textures can all work together if they are combined artfully.

34

Line Flowers...

Focal Flowers...

Line flowers are generally the first flowers placed in the arrangement. They give height to your design and define its perimeter. In addition to tall flowers such as gladioli, the role of line flowers are often filled by branches and tall foliage.

Focal flowers are the most dominant flower in the arrangement. They are typically the flowers you choose first when planning your arrangement, probably because they're your favorites. But you actually insert them (usually) after you insert the line flowers. (In arrangements with lots of flowers, you might have one or more secondary focal flowers.)

Filler flowers are the ones that fill in the empty spaces and add accents of color and texture. They are usually a different shape than the focal flowers and often smaller and more delicate.

Because arrangements differ in size, a particular flower can change roles from one design to another. For example, in a small arrangement irises could be the line flowers (with tulips as the focal flowers); and in a larger arrangement, the irises would be the focal flowers, with bells of Ireland taking over the line flower position.

tips from the pros

No matter how many pieces are in your display, treat each one as an individual—open and form it, manipulate the stems, turn the heads in different directions, and vary the length and angle of each piece.

Work in uneven numbers of flowers to give a dynamic look to the design. With an equal number of flowers, an arrangement could appear static.

Take your time. Your careful attention will prove itself in the grace and energy of the display.

Filler Flowers...

A few roses, lots of tall foliage, stems tied in raffia, a glass container with a medium-sized mouth = a minimalist design in the shape of an inverted triangle, or fan.

Roses mixed with many other flowers of different colors, lots of foliage, a blue glass wide-mouth vase = a casual, contemporary, asymmetrical design.

the same flowers—
different designs

One of the easiest ways to learn how to apply all the aesthetic and practical principles you've seen on paper about arranging flowers is to make several different arrangements with the same core flowers. Here's what we did, using small cream roses.

A mass of closely packed roses, very little foliage, an opaque wide-mouth metal vase = a formal design in the shape of an oval.

about the projects

Ten silk flower designers created the 40 projects for this book, so you'll see a variety of styles and techniques, and a wide range of flowers. In the instructions we list the container first since it sets the personality of an arrangement, then all the floral elements in order of their use. Then come the tools and materials, also in order of their use.

In the design tips we offer ideas on how to modify the design, and interchange flowers, often by season.

We hope that our suggestions are merely that, and that you will study the photos and tips, and then create designs that come from your spirit, to reflect what is important to you and your home. Enjoy!

treasured tiny vases

Take family mementos out of the back of the closet and transform them into treasured vases. For Grandmother's lustrous Japanese egg cups all you need is one flower, such as a delicate apricot anemone.

what you need

Tiny container

Delicate flower

Broad leaf, such as a camellia leaf

what you do

1. Cut the stem short enough so the flower rests on the rim of the container.

2. Cut the broad leaf and insert it underneath the flower.

3. Make a charming arrangement with several vases, or scatter them throughout the house to welcome visiting relatives.

design tips

Thimbles, medicine bottles, salt cellars, old perfume bottles, muffin tins, vintage lipstick holders—just about anything small can become a single-flower vase. Consider miniature poinsettias for holiday arrangements, pansies for spring, and bachelor's buttons for summer. Sweetheart roses and nasturtiums look wonderful any time of the year.

DESIGN BY
SUSAN MCBRIDE

calla lilies in glass

These opulent calla lilies, made of latex, appear wondrously realistic when you apply one of the most basic silk flower design techniques to them—manipulate the stems to imitate the subtle, flowing curves of real flower stems. Display the flowers where they have plenty of room to be admired from all sides.

what you need

Glass vase with wide bottom and narrow mouth

Calla lilies (enough for your design) and saber-like tropical foliage

what you do

1. Angle a few lilies into the vase. Be sure to manipulate the stems so they are slightly curved.

2. Insert a few pieces of tall, pointy foliage deep into the vase. Although real lilies don't have leaves, adding appropriate foliage to the arrangement creates visual variety and also provides a support system for the flower stems.

3. Continue inserting the lilies at an angle into the container. Use as many lilies as is appropriate for your container. We used 11 in this design.

4. Because the flowers are latex, don't place them in direct sunlight—they could start drooping from the heat.

design tips

Big vases with narrow mouths are ideal for busy silk flower arrangers because the vase itself supports the flowers. No need to deal with foam, or vase fillers, or anything else. Other big beauties to consider in such arrangements are amaryllis, birds of paradise, gladioli, and the bold protea.

40

DESIGN BY
CYNTHIA GILLOOLY

single beauties

Sometimes, less is more....

what you do

1. Cut the stems of the daisy-like gerberas so the heights vary by 1 or 2 inches (1.5 cm or 5 cm). If you don't have gerberas, use other perky flowers such as clematis, small sunflowers, or sweet Williams.

2. Place one flower in each vase. Gently bend the stems to give them a more natural appearance.

3. Make an arrangement of the vases. Place them all in a row, perhaps along a mantelpiece or windowsill. Or cluster them on a table or display shelf.

4. Bend the flower heads to work with your composition.

5. Add a subtle surprise as a final touch. Carefully pour water into each vase, slightly varying the levels. (If your flowers are hand-wrapped, delete this step, because the tape will unravel.) Keep the water looking fresh.

6. Stand back and admire how much beauty you created in a few minutes.

design tips

If you'd like to have the illusion of water in your design all the time without having to freshen it, then use what professional silk flower arrangers use—acrylic water. It's rock hard, crystal clear, and very permanent. You can find acrylic water in craft and floral supply stores.

what you need

5 tall, narrow glass bud vases

5 gerberas

Wire cutters

happy lilies of the valley

In the language of flowers favored by Victorian lovers, lilies of the valley symbolized "a return to happiness" because their enchanting spring scent chased away wintry blues. Purple grape hyacinths make pretty partners for the lilies. The demure container accentuates their delicacy.

what you need

Rectangular planter

1 bunch of lilies of the valley, 1 bunch of purple grape hyacinths, 2 bunches of any broad-leafed grass, and moss of any kind

Floral foam, serrated knife, hot-glue gun and glue sticks, wire cutters, green floral wire, and green floral tape

what you do

1. With the serrated knife, cut the floral foam to fit into the planter. Shave the top of the foam with the knife to get a mounded effect. Use a drop of hot glue to secure the foam to the bottom of the planter.

2. Cover the mounded foam with moss, securing it with hot glue.

3. With the wire cutters, cut off the shorter flower stems from the pre-made bunches and shape them into sprays of one, two, or three stems. Stems should be about 4 inches (10.2 cm) long.

4. Arrange each spray with blades of grass or a leaf or two, wrap them with floral wire, and then wrap them again with the floral tape.

5. Gently insert the small sprays into the mounded, moss-covered foam. (Use the photo to guide you.) Fill in any gaps with extra greenery so it all looks lush and abundant.

6. Place the arrangement on a shady windowsill or next to your computer to enjoy "a return to happiness" all year long.

design tips

The beauty of this arrangement is the simple combination of bell-shaped flowers and pointy blades of grass. Any dainty flower could be used, especially small white bell-flowers, larkspur, and tiny penste-mons in all their lovely colors. Choose a container that is muted in color so it doesn't overpower the flowers.

45

daffodil tree with gemstones

Daffodil trumpets joyously announce the first days of spring. Design excitement comes to the monochromatic arrangement from the variety of textures and shapes, including the luminous marble gemstones.

what you do

1. Fill the container about halfway with the marble gemstones. The yellow stones used in this arrangement were chosen to maintain the monochromatic look. If you want a more colorful look, experiment with different colored stones, such as green, clear, or black.

2. Use the scissors, if necessary, to remove any leaves from the daffodil stems except those that are just below the blooms. Place the cluster of daffodils in the center of the gemstones, keeping the stems from touching the sides of the container.

3. Fill in the remainder of the container with the gemstones, being careful not to overfill the container. Leave about 1 inch (2.5 cm) of space from the top of the stones to the mouth of the container.

4. Carefully wrap the ribbon around the stems about 3 inches (7.6 cm) below the blooms. Be sure to place the ribbon straight, keeping it parallel to the top of the container and not leaning askew.

5. Secure the ribbon by simply adding a bead of hot glue, or by pinning it in place with the straight pin.

6. Spread out the greenery and fluff up the daffodils.

design tips

Other flowers that look superb in this monochromatic design are alliums, dahlias, iris, lisianthus, small lilies, tulips, and zinnias. You can use bouquets of multi-colored flowers, too. Vase fillers dramatically alter the mood of a design, so have fun making your own selections. Use anything that coordinates with your flowers, including crystal chips, pebbles, glass cherries, or some other wonderful material.

what you need

Clear container as tall as the flowers

Cluster of daffodils

Marble gemstones and ribbon to match the flowers, scissors or wires cutters, hot-glue gun and glue sticks (or a straight pin)

DESIGN BY

KEN TRUMBAUER

sweetheart wreath

For those who panic at the thought of making wreaths ("I could never make one as fabulous as the ones *she* makes!"), here's a wreath that's perfect for you. It's charming, easy to make, lasts forever, and looks lovely any time of year. In fact, it's such an ideal project, you should gift it to yourself!

what you need

Heart-shaped straw frame

Garlands of wild roses in pink and white

Scissors and U-pins

what you do

1. Cut the rose blossoms and their stems from the two rose garlands. Cut off the leaves and set them aside.

2. Bunch two or three roses between your fingers. Use the U-pins to attach the bunch to the front side of the heart frame. (Don't pin *through* the bunches. Place the prongs of the pins on either side of the bunch.)

3. Continue making bunches and pin them around the frame. As appropriate, insert some leaves every now and then to break up the color of the roses.

4. Fill in the outer and inner edges of the frame with the leaves, attaching them with the U-pins. This may take a while, but by the time you're finished, you'll be so happy with the results, that you'll be eager to start your next wreath.

design tips

We designed this project to be as easy as possible. Continue teaching yourself how to make wreaths by using the same steps in this project, and experimenting with different flowers and foliage. At first, keep things simple, just a few types of flowers (roses of different sizes and medium-size spring flowers are good choices) and a simple color palette. Then expand to more complex projects. For a wreath that's more elaborate (but easy actually), see the *Nature Lover's Herb Wreath* project on page 60.

DESIGN BY
MURIEL EDENS

poppies wrapped in leaves

When you want to recognize a special someone, but you worry that they'd be embarrassed by the gesture, make this friendly arrangement. Leaves cover everyday glassware, and the solitary poppies express simple good wishes. The result is a thoughtful, warm-hearted present.

what you need

3 small juice glasses or votive holders

2 stems of foliage with large leaves, and 3 brightly colored poppies with buds

Hemp, twine, or raffia; hot-glue gun and glue sticks; scissors or wire cutters; serrated knife; and floral foam

50

what to do

1. Choose any large leaves you like, such as dieffenbachia, laurel, magnolia, or salal. Remove the leaves from the foliage stems, trimming off the smaller stems. If the leaves have thick plastic veins in them, trim the veins flat—this makes for easier glueing.

2. Wrapping the leaves around the container gives it an attractive layered disguise. Decorate one vase at a time. Lay the container on its side. Apply a bead of hot glue to the veined side of one of the large leaves and press it to the glass. Roll the leaf a little bit on the side of the glass to spread the glue fully over the leaf. Place the first leaves in the center of the side of the glass and work outwards to the top and bottom.

3. Continue glueing the leaves around the vase, arranging them so you develop a scalloped edge around the top. Parts of the leaves may hang down over the bottom of the container, so just tuck and glue them underneath the container. If needed, use smaller leaves in varying shades of green to patch any areas not covered by the larger leaves.

4. When the vase is covered and cool to the touch, wrap it in several rounds of hemp twine and knot it tightly.

5. With the serrated knife, cut the floral foam to fit and hot glue it to the bottoms of the vases.

6. Arrange the poppies by trimming the stems with the wire cutters so each one mounds up nicely in its vase. Remove all their leaves so only the flowers and their buds are showing.

design tips

Use brightly colored leaves such as variegated pothos, tropical crotans, or burgundy caladium for a dramatic foliage covering. Instead of the poppies, try camellias, nasturtiums, or ranunculus—any kind of flower that will mound prettily above the leaf wrapping.

DESIGN BY
SUSAN McBRIDE

french country flowers

One of the greatest achievements of a floral design is to look as if it hasn't been designed at all, as if you just carried the flowers in from the garden and stuck them in a handy container. The spontaneous look requires a liberal use of space between the flowers and a container with a laissez-faire attitude.

52

what you need

Tall, sturdy container, very wide at the top, such as a French floral bucket

Enough stems of blue delphinium, lupine, white delphinium, and bells of Ireland to fill your container

Serrated knife, floral foam, and scissors or wire cutters

what to do

1. With the knife, cut the floral foam to fit bottom of container.

2. Fluff out all the leaves and petals of the flowers. Insert the stalks of the blue delphinium as if they were spokes in a half-circle hub. Some will be at the top, others will be drooping gently out of the sides. Cut the stalks if necessary, as you go, so their heights will vary nicely in the arrangement. Notice that the arrangement has an unequal number (five) of open spaces between the flower bunches. If the flowers were closely packed together, the arrangement would take on a more formal, traditional look.

3. Use one of the white delphiniums as the spoke on one of the sides to give the arrangement a dynamic, slightly asymmetrical look.

4. Sparingly add the lupine, which is usually shorter than the delphiniums.

5. Add the rest of the white delphiniums where needed for a balance of strong white color.

6. Add the green bells of Ireland for a length of shapely green.

7. Bend stems at the side where needed. Resist the urge to primp things too much. Leave everything a little wild.

design tips

For an elegant look, make the same arrangement and place it in a vase of china or silver. Gladioli, hollyhocks, and iris are other wonderful flowers to choose. And don't think you have to use only flowers—long sword-like leaves, pussy willows, branches with berries, cattails, and high grasses are terrific elements in fan-shaped arrangements.

DESIGN BY

MURIEL EDENS

slender inspiration

Though he's never been to Japan, the designer of this project has been greatly inspired by Japanese art and philosophy. Notice how all the elements of the design interact with one another—the delicate shapes of the plants, the glazed finish of the shallow container, the variety of textures, and the marvelous use of space. To accentuate the design's simple beauty, surround it with lots of natural light.

what you need

Flat container, such as a large sushi dish

3 dendrobium orchids, 3 curly willow branches, 3 fiddler ferns, and sphagnum moss

Serrated knife, floral foam, hot-glue gun and glue sticks

54

what you do

1. With the serrated knife, cut the floral foam to fit the sushi dish, and then hot glue it to the top of the dish.

2. Although the arrangement is open to all sides, it's really designed to have a front and back. So decide where your front is and work from there. Notice that the designer used three pieces of the three different elements, so think in terms of pleasingly balanced threes. For example, the orchids are placed in the center back, but each has a different height.

3. Insert the curly willow branches around the orchids, in another pleasing threesome.

4. Insert the fiddler ferns in the back and on the two sides, leaving the front open so you can see all the plants interacting with one another.

5. Add the moss, piece by piece. Hot glue it to the foam so it's strong and stable.

6. Place the arrangement where its front side will be the one facing the viewer.

design tips

Experimenting with Ikebana-influenced designs is a wonderful way to learn how to use tall, graceful plants, including slender foliage, branches of all kinds, and delicate flowers such as broom, forsythia, foxglove, larkspur, and mallow. When deciding on combinations, let your innate sense of balance and harmony be your guide.

DESIGN BY

TOM METCALF

may basket

Children used to "bring in the May" with a tradition that dates back to the Celtic holiday of Beltane. They would hang baskets filled with flowers and sweets on neighbors' doorknobs, knock loudly, then run away giggling before each door was opened. Make this lacy May basket, filled with lavender hydrangea, to bring a smile to anyone on your secret gift list.

what you need

Cotton lace doily, 7 inches (17.8 cm) in diameter

1 large round stem of purple hydrangea and 5 to 7 large green leaves with stems

Polystyrene foam cone (7 inches [17.8 cm] long), serrated knife, corsage pins, floral wire, wire cutter, green floral tape, and ribbon in a color to match the flowers

what you do

1. You can find brand-new lace doilies in craft stores. If you want to use a vintage doily, hand wash and starch it to make it more sturdy.

2. With the serrated knife, cut 1½ inches (3.8 cm) off the pointed end of the cone. Then with a firm straight cut, shear off about 1½ inches (3.8 cm) on one long side of the cone to get a flat edge. This will make the cone lie flat against a wall or door when it is hanging.

3. Fold over the top quarter of the lace doily and wrap the doily around the cone. Secure it in the back with the corsage pins so it fits snugly. Lacy bits should hang down completely, covering the pointy end. If needed, use the serrated knife to trim the cone to fit the doily.

4. Cut the stem of the hydrangea to about 4 inches (10.2 cm). Insert it into the center of the broad end of the cone, pushing it all the way down so it's held securely.

5. Wrap the stems of the leaves with wire, and then with the floral tape. Insert the leaves around the hydrangea flowers to surround them with a collar that hides the foam.

6. With a ribbon cut to length, make the handle on the back flat side of the basket. Use the corsage pins to secure the ends of the ribbon on opposite sides of the basket. If you wish, cut and add other ribbons for decoration.

7. On May 1st leave your basket on the door of someone you love, but don't get caught making the delivery!

design tips

May baskets, of course, can be made and given away any time the fancy strikes you. Roses are always beautiful in lacy containers, and so are camellias, lilacs, ranunculus, and tulips. Have fun with a basket made of neon-glow felt and fill it with zingy flowers, such as orange day lilies, radiant sunflowers, crimson fuschias, or magenta zinnias.

DESIGN BY

SUSAN MCBRIDE

sunflower radiance

Native Americans have been using wild sunflowers as food and medicine for at least 8,000 years. When it was introduced to Europe, the sunflower was considered an amazing curiosity, since it's the only single flower that can grow as much as 11 inches (28 cm) a week! Celebrate sizzling days and lightning-bug nights with the radiant symbol of summertime.

58

what you need

1. With the serrated knife, cut the floral foam to fit the bottom of the container.

2. With the wire cutters, separate the individual flowers from their bunches.

3. Insert the largest flowers first to give form to the arrangement.

4. Fill in the arrangement with the smaller sunflowers.

design tips

Other summer-signature flowers are black-eyed Susans, buttercups, clematis, coneflowers, gerberas, magnolias, phlox, and yarrow. They each look fabulous when combined in glorious numbers.

what you need

Sturdy, wide container

Bunches of sunflowers, various sizes, enough to fit your container

Serrated knife, floral foam, and wire cutters or scissors

DESIGN BY
MURIEL EDENS

nature lover's herb wreath

The unique elements in this generous wreath are herbs—long thin spikes of lavender and short yellow blooms of chamomile. How different! How lovely!

what you need

Oval (or round) straw wreath, 12 inches (30.5 cm) wide

10 pieces of cedar with berries, several lengths of ivy (2 to 12 inches [5 to 30.5 cm] long), 4 bunches of lavender, 3 eucalyptus branches, and 2 chamomile bunches

U-pins and floral wire

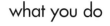

60

DESIGN BY
ROGER BALLEW

what you do

1. If you use an oval wreath, turn it so the longer dimension is horizontal. To make a hanger, wrap the wire several times around the top of the wreath; make a loop and twist the pieces of wire together, tucking any loose ends into the back of the wreath.

2. Using the U-pins, cover the front and sides of the wreath with the cedar and ivy. Place the cedar in one direction. Place the ivy in both directions.

3. Place two of the eucalyptus branches on the front bottom of the wreath, reaching out in opposite directions. Cut the remaining branches into smaller pieces about 6 inches (15.2 cm) long and insert them throughout the wreath.

4. Wire nine to 13 pieces of lavender into a bunch, making six bunches. In a fan pattern cascading downward, insert three bunches on each side of the bottom front of the wreath, nestling them among the eucalyptus. (Use the photo to guide you.)

5. Insert about 10 pieces of lavender on each side of the bottom half, sticking them out front a bit for dramatic effect. Fill in any blank spaces on the bottom middle section with the remaining pieces.

6. Insert herbs as appropriate all over the rest of the wreath, going in the same one-way direction as the cedar. On the bottom, insert the herbs pointing both ways (as you did with the ivy) and also out to the sides.

7. Cut the bunches of chamomile into individual stems. Place some of them in the bottom half of the wreath to cover the ends of the lavender.

8. Place the remainder of the chamomile into the rest of wreath as you did with the lavender. Fill in spaces with any of the remaining materials as you wish.

9. We decided to resist the urge to trim the wayward pieces on the wreath because we loved its natural, wild look. If you want your wreath a little more tamed, then create more space in the center and cut your lavender bunches shorter so they don't poke their heads out so far.

design tips

The easiest way to modify the wreath to your color palette is to merely replace the lavender and the chamomile and keep every other element. Instead of purple and yellow accents, you could have blue and pink, or silver and white—or any other color combination you like.

mad hatter's tea party

Who says flower designs always have to be elegant and sophisticated? How about zingy and whimsical? With tulips, spider mums, and daisies, a crayon-colored tea set becomes a playful table display.

what you need

Brightly colored teapot and teacups

Spider mums, yellow and orange tulips, and daisies

Serrated knife and floral foam

what you do for the teapot

1. Use the serrated knife to cut and shape floral foam inside the teapot.

2. Insert the larger flowers, the spider mums, first. Work in uneven numbers, such as five and seven, for a stronger design. Cut the stems as you go along, but be sure to leave enough stem—you can always cut them shorter if you need to. Use the photograph to guide you, arranging the flowers higher at the top and shorter at the bottom, forming a full mound.

3. Insert the tulips so the two different colors are seen clearly.

4. Fill in any negative spaces to create an abundant look.

5. Add moss to any areas that the flowers don't cover. Don't make it too neat; it looks more enticing with a natural appearance.

what you do for the teacups

1. Use the serrated knife to cut a section of foam to fill the teacup.

2. Cut off the heads of the daisies, leaving a 2-inch (5 cm) stem. Insert the daisies in a row around the mouth of the cup, so their heads are peaking outward.

3. Cut off the tulip heads, again leaving a 2-inch (5 cm) stem. Insert them into the center of the teacup, standing straight up. Because the flowers are placed so tightly, no moss is needed.

4. Add several more teacups to balance the whole arrangement. Follow steps 1 to 2 above, just using daisies.

design tips

Gather a collection of vintage teacups and saucers that have been orphaned from their sets. Add a lovely teapot. Put them all together with flowers that smooth over differences, such as sweetheart roses or small peonies.

DESIGN BY

KEN TRUMBAUER

sylvan wall sconce

This unique wall sconce re-creates an afternoon the designer spent in a wild meadow, when she came upon a bird's nest hidden in the flowers. Memories are often the inspiration for a design. And making memories is what happens when we assemble flowers and other accessories into an arrangement we can admire for a long time. This design is a simple combination of foliage, grass, berries—and that unforgettable nest.

what you need

Foam cone (12 inches [30.5 cm] long

3 stems of leafy greenery, 3 stems of tall grass (colors can vary), 2 stems of asparagus fern, 3 canes of raspberries, 1 grapevine nest and eggs, and sphagnum moss

Serrated knife, wire cutters or scissors, green floral wire, hot-glue gun and glue sticks

what you do

1. With the serrated knife, shear off about 1½ inches (3.8 cm) from one side of the cone to flatten it so it will rest flush against the wall. This leaves a half-moon shape on the top, where you'll insert the flower stems.

2. Here's how to wrap the cone with leaves: With the scissors, remove the leaves from the leafy greenery, cutting off the stems. On a flat surface, arrange the leaves from larger to smaller. Starting at the rim of the cone, at the flat end, wrap the first row with the largest leaves. Glue the top of the leaves, but let the pointed tips remain unglued.

3. Wrap the second row, tucking the leaves underneath the pointed tips in the row above and glueing them down. Continue wrapping the leaves in rows around the cone to completely hide the foam and give structure to the sconce.

4. Once you have completely covered the sconce, choose five to seven leaves of contrasting color from the canes of raspberries, and glue these onto the top rim to create a pleasing rim for your floral arrangement.

5. On the flat side of the sconce, in the center toward the top, deeply insert a length of folded wire to fashion a hanging hook. Secure it with glue and then glue plenty of leaves over it to reinforce it.

6. On the flat end of the half-moon shape of the sconce, insert the tall grasses, fanning them out dramatically. (Don't hesitate to give them a haircut if they're too unruly.)

7. In front of the grasses, insert the ferns, so they add volume but don't reach as high as the grasses.

8. On the rounded edge, insert the berry canes, which will be taller than the ferns, but not as high as the grasses. Turn and twist the canes to show off the colorful berries.

9. Hot glue the little eggs into the nest. Use the floral tape or the wire to attach the nest to the berry canes, so it rests at a natural level position. Hide the cone base with moss, using hot glue if necessary.

design tips

Create an autumn sconce with burgundy and amber leaves and beige and brown grasses. For weddings, use foliage sprayed white and gold, with branches of beautiful snowberries. For the holidays, use poinsettia petals as the leaves and fill the sconce with branches, grasses, and winterberries.

65

DESIGN BY

SUSAN MCBRIDE

magnolias in cobalt blue

Fresh magnolia flowers last only about a day, so what a pleasure it is to enjoy their southern charm in silk for as long as you like. Being magnolias, they look magnificent in any kind of container. Put them in a cobalt blue glass vase—and they become positively breathtaking.

what you need

Cobalt blue vase with a wide bottom and narrow mouth

3 large white magnolias

Scissors or wire cutters

what you do

1. Cut the bottom leaves off the stems, leaving just a few underneath the magnolia blooms.

2. Cut the stems in three different heights. Arrange the flowers so they are facing slightly different directions. (Use the photo to guide you.)

3. Arrange the leaves underneath the flowers to fill in the space gracefully. The vase's narrow mouth firmly holds the flower stems, so you don't need anything else to maintain the shape of the arrangement— what could be easier?

4. Display the flowers where you want to create a touch of southern elegance and a dash of dramatic beauty.

design tips

All flowers look wonderful in cobalt blue vases, so you can never go wrong with a collection of them in different sizes and shapes. Other big beauties for large arrangements include amaryllis, pom-pom chrysanthemums, and peonies. To create a southern garden theme, use azaleas, black-eyed Susans, purple coneflowers, crape myrtle, day lilies, dogwood blossoms, geraniums, or hydrangeas.

DESIGN BY

SUSAN McBRIDE

english cottage garden

This seemingly casual design is actually a study in grace and beauty. To achieve the look, divide the fan-shaped arrangement into zones, such as the central zone, the side zones, and the lower zone, as the designer did. Once you learn this principle, you can easily emulate the design in an endless variety of different flowers.

what you need

Rectangular basket

Spanish moss, 3 purple agapanthus, 2 blue delphiniums, 4 hot pink gerberas, 2 mauve sedums, 3 white lisianthus, 5 waxflower foliage stems, grass-like foliage, and strappy foliage (such as dracaena leaves or ti leaves)

Serrated knife, floral foam, and scissors

what you do

1. With the serrated knife, cut the floral foam to fit snugly in the basket.

2. Cover the floral foam with the Spanish moss.

3. Place three purple agapanthus into the central zone of the design.

4. Place one stem of blue delphinium at the top of the arrangement. Cut the second stem in half and place it so that it emerges from the central zone of the design. Place the other half of the stem on the bottom right of the arrangement.

5. Insert the gerberas.

6. Add the mauve sedums to the design.

7. Cut each of the lisianthus stems into two sections. Flesh out the shape of the design by interspersing them to create the bottom horizontal lines of the arrangement. Place the remaining lisianthus blossoms throughout the design.

8. Cut the waxflower foliage into separate florets and insert them as filler throughout the framework of the design.

9. Insert the grass and strappy foliage, filling in any spots that need to be covered.

design tips

Notice how the flowers in this arrangement are in the cool colors of blue, purple, mauve, and wild pink, with a dash of white. Compare them to the warmer hues in the *Sophisticated Combination* project on page 94. If you study both these projects and imagine substituting the flowers with your own choices, you'll be giving yourself an excellent silk flower design class.

68

lilac nostalgia

Lilacs were introduced to Europe from their homeland in the mountains around Istanbul in the 1500s. Ever since, the beautiful and fragrant spring-blooming flower has been a favorite in gardens the world over, including, no doubt, a garden from your childhood. Revel in a bit of lilac nostalgia with this appealing display that loves leaves as much as flowers.

what you need

Clean, galvanized bucket

Lilacs (enough to fill your container) and sheet moss

Floral foam, serrated knife, and scissors or wire cutters

what you do

1. Fill the bucket with floral foam. Use the serrated knife to shape it, so it fits snugly into the bucket.

2. Cut the lilac stems so they're all the same length. Fluff up all the flowers and leaves.

3. Start in the center of the bucket and insert the lilacs in a straight and upright position. Keep all the heads of the flowers at about the same level.

4. Fill the base around the flowers with sheet moss. You can wet the moss to achieve a snug fit around the flowers.

design tips

With a design this easy, you can use about any tall flower you want. Consider orchids, gayfeather, or globe amaranth for an unconventional look, and chrysanthemums, iris, fuchsia, or grape hyacinth for something more traditional. If you don't have a galvanized tin bucket, use a sand pail or a terra-cotta pot.

DESIGN BY
KEN TRUMBAUER

ferns from the forest

Although it's a monochromatic design, the variety of shades of green, shapes, and textures gives the display an exhilarating realism. Just looking at it makes you feel as cool as if you were indeed walking along a path in a shady forest, the fern fronds brushing against your face. Oh, the incredible pleasure of green…

what you need

Old clay pot

Medium-size Boston fern, bird nest fern, bunch of button fern, green sheet moss, and angel vine

Hot-glue gun and glue sticks, floral foam

what you do

1. Hot glue the floral foam to the pot just below the rim.

2. Insert the Boston fern into the middle of the pot.

3. Insert the bird nest fern and the button fern on opposite sides.

4. Shape and bend the ferns to make them look natural.

5. Cover the bottom of the display with green moss, then glue a small piece of moss to the side of clay pot.

6. Spread the angel vine delicately over the ferns.

design tips

One of the most interesting ways to make silk flower arrangements look real is to use containers that show signs of age, such as the clay pot with lichen used in this project. Other such containers are aged wooden boxes (such as soda pop bottle carriers), old maple syrup buckets, vintage cigar boxes, and baskets made of wire, bark or branches. Instead of ferns, use whatever plant material is appropriate for the size of the container—such as a variety of grasses or a collection of branches and berries. For flowers, choose an assortment suitable for a country look, such as asters, cosmos, daisies, freesia, mums, Queen Anne's Lace, and poppies.

DESIGN BY

LUCK McELREATH

positive peonies

The spectacular beauty of the peony makes it the supreme flower in Chinese symbolism. According to the ancient traditions of Feng Shui (the art of harmonious placement), peonies cause a positive flow of *chi*, or energy. To ensure you'll experience their beneficial effects as often as possible, place peonies where they will catch your eye every day.

what you need

Vase to hold big flowers

Large white peonies and 2 stalks of foliage with long, wide leaves, such as hydrangea or viburnum leaves

what you do

1. Cut the peonies to fit into the vase, removing all the leaves. Insert the flowers so they create a lush, abundant mound. Arrange them close together, as in the photograph, for a traditional look. If you want a more casual look, use fewer flowers so there is more space between them. Bend down one flower near the center for balance.

2. Cut two lengths of the foliage and insert them so they droop gracefully on the sides. Don't use the peony leaves; they don't have the nice swoop you want for this design.

design tips

Any multi-petal flowers, including roses, look wonderful in full mounds, so feel free to experiment with your favorites. Complement the flowers with an elegant container, perhaps a luminous one like the vintage bamboo-style vase we used. To accentuate an Asian connection, use flowers that are treasured by the Chinese, such as azaleas, chrysanthemums, narcissus, and water lilies, or branches with plum or cherry blossoms.

DESIGN BY

SUSAN McBRIDE

fairy princess crown wreath

Fairies love dressing up and dancing all night long to the music played on their fairy pipes. They are especially proud of their crown wreaths, made of tiny, pastel flowers they've gathered from the meadows after sunrise. Here's a wreath to fashion for your favorite fairy princess.

what you need

Spool wire

1 stem of multiple bluebells, 1 stem of multiple wild spray roses (your choice of color), 1 stem of lavender montellia, 2 stems of multiple small daisies, 1 stem of white mustard berry, 1 stem of multiple blue waxflowers, and 1 stem of feather-like fern

Measuring tape, 1 yd. (.9 m) each of pink, lavender, and moss green sheer ribbon, spool wire, green floral tape, and wire cutters

what you do

1. Measure the head size of the fairy princess who will be wearing the crown wreath, then add another 1½ inches (3.8 cm) on both ends. Cut the wire to that length, so it will be long enough to connect the ends when the wreath is finished.

2. Clip all the flower stems so they have just enough stem left to connect them to the wire. (We used the flowers listed, but you can use any small flowers you like.) Save the stems to add length to flowers in other arrangements. Cut the fern, the stems of lavender montellia and the berries into small pieces. Sort all the flowers so it's easy to find and pick up each one when you need it.

3. About 1½ inches (3.8 cm) from one end of the wire, tape a piece of fern to the wire, and then tape one of each of the flowers. Make sure the colors are mixed pleasingly and are spaced apart evenly from one

another. Don't put the flowers too close together or the wreath will get too thick. It looks best when it's a little airy. Repeat about every 1½ inches (3.8 cm) until you're close to the end.

4. Wrap the last 1½ inches (3.8 cm) of wire with the floral tape. Loop the two ends of the wire together like a chain and weave the ends around the base of the wreath.

5. Make bows with the three ribbons. Wrap floral tape around pieces of wire, gather the bows and wire each one to the back of the wreath. Tug any loose pieces into the wreath, or use a pencil to curl them like tendrils of vine. Keep long streamers on the ribbons so they'll fly around gleefully when the fairies are dancing.

design tips

Make wreaths for boys (who, alas, might be too shy for flowers) out of different shades and shapes of leaves, with a few berries. Anytime you want a bit of magic and a nighttime of dancing, make a wreath for yourself and your merry-making friends. Follow the same directions, just make the wreath bigger and feel free to use bolder flowers.

DESIGN BY
SUSAN PARTAIN

sunny tuscany

Imagine yourself in a villa in Tuscany, on the west coast of Italy facing the lovely Tyrrhenian Sea. Everywhere in sight is a riot of gorgeous color: the ancient burnt sienna walls, the royal blue shutters, the deep green on the distant mountains, and the hundreds of scented flowers cascading down the garden terraces. Ah, Tuscany!

what you need

2 terra-cotta pots, 1 large, 1 small

Grape leaves with grapes and vines, 5 twig sprays, 8 grass bunches, 22 bunches of various sizes of rust-colored chrysanthemums, 22 stems of large pale yellow yarrow, and 5 brown-tipped fiddler ferns

Wire cutters, serrated knife, floral foam, floral wire, and thick wire, such as a coat hanger

what you do

1. With the wire cutters, cut away the vines from the main stem of the grape leaves.

2. With the serrated knife, cut the floral foam so it fits snugly into the bottom of the large pot.

3. Make the twigs look like vines by twisting them or curling them around your fingers. Wrap them around the mouth of the big pot, letting some twigs droop down on one side. It will look like a mess at this point, but don't get discouraged!

4. Place the small terra-cotta pot inside the large pot. Secure it by wrapping the thick wire around the bottom of the pot and inserting the ends in the foam.

5. Stick the grass bunches into the front of the foam in the large pot, so the small pot seems to be lying in a bed of grass.

6. Place two grape bunches on vines into the small pot. Insert their stems through the drainage hole of the small pot into the foam in the large pot.

7. To create the base of your design, arrange some of the grapevine and twigs on the top of the big pot. Use small pieces of grapevine to cover the outer rim of the mouth of the large pot and cover the floral foam.

8. Insert the chrysanthemums into the center of the large pot. Place them at different heights so they can show themselves off.

9. Insert the yarrow flowers throughout the design, the taller ones in the center, the shorter ones at the sides. Cut the stems as needed.

10. Insert the ferns as tall filler.

11. Fluff up everything as if it had just stopped swaying in the sea breeze.

design tips

Sun-drenched displays beg to be duplicated, so go ahead. The pot-within-a-pot design gives you lots of options for unique accents. For any of the ingredients, substitute flowers, fruits, and foliage from your own color palette. Use the photograph and the sequence of the instructions above to guide you.

78

DESIGN BY
ROGER BALLEW

simply exotic

The elements are simple: a sky-reaching branch, a cluster of mandarin red amaryllis, a single bold leaf, and lots of surrounding space. The result is an Ikebana-inspired statement of grace and subtle power. Place the arrangement in a brightly lit area that is otherwise unadorned, so it can have the center-stage attention it deserves.

what you need

Contemporary container

1 tall piece of curly willow branch, 1 big green leaf, 3 red amaryllis (or other dramatic flower), dried leaves or pods, and moss

Floral tape, floral foam, hot-glue gun and glue sticks, and U-pins

what you do

1. Hot glue the floral foam to the inside of the vase so it fits snugly.

2. Insert the curly willow branch into the foam slightly left of center. (Notice in the photo how the height and dramatic shape of the branch balances the weight of the bright red amaryllis cluster.)

3. Place the big leaf on the other side, cutting its stem if necessary so the leaf is half or less the height of the curly willow. (Use the photo to guide you.)

4. Clip short the stems of the amaryllis and bundle them together with the floral tape. Insert the bundle into the foam just at the bottom of the design facing front center.

5. Give the flowers more drama by duplicating the shape of their petals in another medium, such as dried leaves. Insert them sparingly into the foam underneath the flowers.

6. Use U-pins to neatly cover the bottom of the arrangement with moss. Add another touch or two of curly willow if you feel it's needed.

design tips

A vase with a rich, reflective glaze adds a gleam to the whole arrangement. Instead of amaryllis, you can use other show-off flowers such as daylilies, hibiscus, cabbage roses, or giant zinnias. For an arrangement that is equally elegant but more modest, use pink azaleas, pale peonies, white calla lilies, or even a solitary bird of paradise.

80

DESIGN BY
LUCK McELREATH

gracious tower

This tall, gracious design captures the mood of autumn with the use of only four elements of different heights. Since the back and sides are finished as well, you can set the arrangement in front of a mirror to give an ordinary space a big dose of personality. Or place it on a pedestal to be the focal point of an entire wall.

what you need

Big, sturdy rectangular container

1 bunch of very tall wild grass, 2 sprays of bittersweet, 1 autumn Japanese maple branch, and 6 latex apples

1 brick of floral foam, adhesive floral clay or hot-glue gun and glue sticks, scissors or wire cutters, and floral picks

what you do

1. Securely attach the foam to the container with the adhesive floral clay or hot glue.

2. Cut stems of wild grass from the pre-made bunch and insert them into the middle of the foam, spreading and shaping them to create a natural look.

3. Cut the bittersweet sprays into individual pieces. Beginning with the tallest pieces, insert them all around the grass bunch, in a "stair-step" placement, so the pieces graduate "out and down" as they get shorter.

4. Curve six of the smaller pieces of bittersweet in the same direction and insert them around the base of the grass and the vertical bittersweet pieces.

5. Cut the Japanese maple branch into short clusters, and insert them deep into the foam at the bottom of the design.

6. Glue the apples onto picks, some at the stem end and some at the bottom. Place them at different heights and angles around the bottom of the design, deep into the Japanese maple leaves.

design tips

Create a lively summer look with green grasses, summer-leafed Japanese maple branches or bamboo, with flowers of rhododendron or wisteria. For the winter holidays, combine bare branches with berry branches, and add clusters of evergreens and pomegranates. For spring, combine pussy willows and branches of forsythia, or spring blooms such as peach, plum, and apple.

DESIGN BY

BETH HOHENSEE

mini-xeriscape

Succulents and sedums are some of the newest artificial plants to come on the market. Both are favorites in live xeriscape gardens, designed for earth-friendly, low water usage. Enjoy the desert-at-twilight palette of this no-fuss display that looks as interesting from the side as it does from the top.

what you need

Low, round container

"Hens and Chicks" succulent, and the brown flower of a sedum

Serrated knife, floral foam, river pebbles, and gravel

what you do

1. With the serrated knife, cut the floral foam to fit snugly into the container.

2. Sprinkle the top of the foam lightly with the gravel.

3. Place the succulent into the container slightly left of center. Cut the stem of the sedum flower and insert it into the foam. (Use the photo to guide your placement.)

4. Place the pebbles around the two plants and fill in any bare spots with the gravel.

design tips

Succulents and sedums are growing in popularity, so you should be able to find an ample selection of these fascinating plants in floral and craft supply stores. When making larger arrangements, be adventurous in your choice of "ground cover" and consider materials such cypress or bark mulch, colored sand, or broken pieces of terra-cotta.

84

DESIGN BY

SUSAN MCBRIDE

rock simplicity

One of the most exciting aspects of working with silk florals is the chance to create beautiful displays with plants that you may never combine in real life. Horsetails are flowerless plants that grow in wet, boggy places. Many bromeliads, on the other hand, are "air plants," able to absorb most of their nutrients without being planted in soil. From this odd couple, the designer made a stunning display.

what you need

Rock or other base object

3 to 5 stalks of horsetails and a matching number of bromeliads

Hot-glue gun and glue sticks, and flower frog

what you do

1. Hot glue the flower frog into a drilled rock (such as a votive candle rock) or other form suitable for using as a base for your arrangement. (Or use a pre-assembled frog and base from a specialty garden shop.)

2. Insert three to five stalks of the horsetails onto the center spikes of the frog. Vary the heights around the tallest horsetail.

3. Place the bromeliads on the outside spikes of the frog, forming a circular hedge around the horsetail.

4. If you wish, make a plantscape by surrounding the display with light colored sand and gravel.

design tips

You can turn any solid rock into an exciting base for silk plants by drilling a hole into it the size and shape of the flower frog you want it to hold. Create different designs by using bamboo stalks and wild grasses, or berry branches and wildflowers.

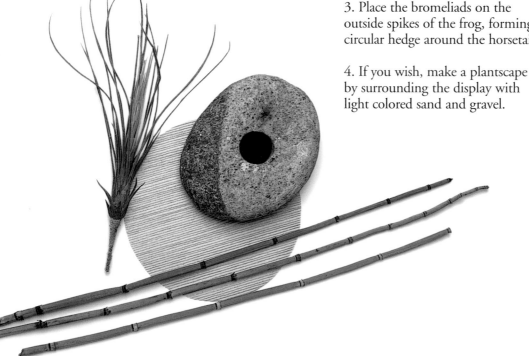

DESIGN BY

TOM METCALF

subtle autumn swag

The palette of this late-season swag is diverse yet subtle—yellow, purple, peach, and brown, with green from the leaves of ivy. Festoon a doorway or window, drape a mantel, or show it off on a long table as the centerpiece for an abundant autumn feast.

what you need

2 bamboo poles, 24 inches (61 cm)

2 ivy garlands (5 feet [1.5 m] in length, 1 with small leaves, 1 with medium leaves), 1 grapevine garland with large leaves and clusters of grapes, 8 stalks brown eucalyptus, 2 large stalks purple Veronica or other spiky purple flowers, 2 large stalks of small pale yellow and peach yarrow, 7 large bright yellow yarrow, and 1 bouquet of tiny yellow chamomile flowers (or small daisy centers)

Floral wire, pre-cut into pieces, 6 inches (15.2 cm) long, green and brown floral tape, and wire cutters

88

what you do

1. Create a structure for the swag by wiring together the bamboo poles into the shape of a broad "X." Wrap floral tape around the poles about 3 inches (7.5 cm) on either side of where they intersect to strengthen the center.

2. Using the pre-cut wire pieces, attach the small-leaf ivy garland to the bamboo "X." Start at one end and wind it to the other end, stopping to wire every 4 inches (10.2 cm) or so. Repeat with the medium-size ivy garland. Lastly, wind the grape vine; arrange the grapes in a symmetrical fashion and let the leaves hang down slightly to enhance the feeling of abundance.

3. Trim four of the eucalyptus stalks to varying lengths. Wire them closely together just past the center of the swag on the right side. Repeat with the remaining stalks for the left side.

4. On top of the eucalyptus, wire the stalks of purple Veronica flowers. Manipulate the flower stems to look more natural. When wiring flowers onto the swag, hide the wire behind and beneath the ivy leaves. Cut and twist the ends of the wire to the backside of the swag and bend them flat. This looks prettier and it's safer to handle the swag when you know all the ends are on one side.

5. Cut the stems of the small peach and yellow yarrow flowers into lengths of 4 inches (10.2 cm). Wire them in throughout the swag, adding color and volume.

6. The center of this arrangement is the focal point. Make a small, tight bouquet with five of the big yellow yarrow flowers and their greenery. Cut the stems to a length of 4 inches (10.2 cm), wire and tape them together, and then wire the entire bouquet into the center of the swag. Add the remaining two big yellow yarrow flowers, one each on the center of each top arm of the "X."

7. Cut the tiny chamomile flowers from its bouquet and wire each one throughout the swag. This final touch adds unity to the color palette.

design tips

It's easy to make a similar swag in different colors. For example, our swag has the spiky colors from one side of the color chart (purple) and all the other flowers from the other side of the chart (yellow/peach). You could partner teal and cream/apricot/white, for example, for a stunning spring look. Or make a super-sophisticated swag by going monochromatic, with white and cream for all the flowers and the palest of pale green for the foliage. See the *Wintry Centerpiece* on page 106 for subtle color combinations for winter holidays

DESIGN BY
SUSAN McBRIDE

bronze chrysanthemums

You don't need many mums to celebrate their beauty. With Asian-style spareness, all you need are a few of them, plus some greenery and grasses, and a solid earthy vase. With those minimal elements—and a lot of space—you can capture the spirit of the quintessential autumn flower.

what you need

Sturdy, elegant container with a wide mouth

Tall wild grass, curly willow twig with beautiful long curves, 2 long stems of bronze chrysanthemums, 1 bunch of short bronze chrysanthemums, 2 bunches of bear grass, and green sheet moss

Hot-glue gun and glue sticks, and floral foam

what you do

1. Hot glue the foam into the container, making sure that it fits snugly.

2. Insert the tall grass and the curly willow twig into the middle of the foam.

3. Bend and shape the two tall bronze mums and place them on opposite sides of the grass and twig so they face each other, at slightly different levels. (See the photo to guide you.) Remove most of the leaves to create a spare look on the stems.

4. Cut the short mums and insert them around the bottom of the tall mums.

5. Insert the two bunches of bear grass. Arrange one bunch on one side so it lounges downward and the opposite bunch so that it reaches upward, creating balance between the two.

6. Spread moss around the bottom of the arrangement so it hangs naturally.

design tips

Any kind of flower with lots of petals, such as dahlias, lilacs, peonies, or medium-sized sunflowers, would look remarkable with this spare arrangement. In a narrow-mouthed vase, just eliminate the bottom flowers and let the two single stems rise gloriously by themselves. For shorter arrangements, use the same principles with more diminutive flowers such as asters, carnations, Lenten roses, or marigolds placed at slightly different levels.

DESIGN BY
LUCK McELREATH

sassy pomanders

In medieval times, pomander balls were filled with sweet-smelling herbs and spices that ladies placed in their handkerchiefs to sniff when they wanted to avoid awful smells. Later, ribbons were added and pomanders became bouquets and hanging ornaments popular at the holidays. Today pomanders are look-at-me décor accents—all are classy, some are classy and sassy.

what you need

Polystyrene foam balls, 3 to 5 inches (7.6 to 12.7 cm) in diameter

6 bunches of orange, cream, and yellow roses

Serrated knife (optional), scissors, hot-glue gun and glue sticks

what you do

1. Flatten the bottom of a foam ball so it will sit securely on a table, either by smacking the ball on a tabletop or slicing off the bottom with the serrated knife.

2. Cut the flower heads off the stems.

3. Starting at the middle of the ball, hot glue the flower heads to the ball in a circular pattern until the surface of the ball is completely covered. Make the rest of your pomanders in the same way.

4. If you're in a gloriously excessive mood, place all your pomanders in a show-off circle like we did, or line them up in a row down the center of a table. Make smaller pomanders for the lucky ones on your no-reason-at-all-except-you're-wonderful gift list.

design tips

We made pomanders with one kind of flower to show you how easy they are to make. Do consider more elaborate designs. Impress everyone at the wedding with fantastic centerpiece pomanders in white, cream, and apricot sweetheart roses. Other terrific pomander flowers are anemones, camellias, dahlias, daisies, and pansies.

92

DESIGN BY
CYNTHIA GILLOOLY

sophisticated combination

Summery orange poppies and green bells of Ireland with autumnal velvety brown cattails and jaunty golden berries—what a sensational combination. With the addition of a wasp nest and lichen, this sophisticated arrangement becomes touchingly realistic. With the distinctive copper container, it glows.

what you need

Sturdy copper container

Spanish moss, 2 bells of Ireland stems, 3 cattails, 2 orange poppy stems, 3 golden berry stems, wasp nest, lichen, and strappy leaf foliage

Serrated knife, floral foam, scissors, hot-glue gun and glue sticks

what you do

1. With the serrated knife, cut the floral foam to fit snugly into the container.

2. Cover the foam with the Spanish moss.

3. Insert the bells of Ireland as the highest element in the design.

4. Insert the cattails in the center at the top, then on the left, then the right. (Use the photo to guide you.)

5. Cut the individual poppy stems from the main stems and insert them into the design, from top to bottom. Be sure to manipulate the stems so they look natural.

6. Cut the golden berry stems into sections and intersperse them throughout the design. Let several droop down nicely at the sides near the bottom.

7. Add the strappy foliage so it seems to reach out all around the design.

8. Hot glue the wasp nest and lichen into the base.

design tips

You can make just a few substitutions and change the entire look of this arrangement. For example, use pussy willows instead of cattails, pink snapdragons instead of bells of Ireland, red holly berries instead of gold berries. Use different accessories such as a bird nest, butterflies, driftwood, dried lotus pods or pinecones.

DESIGN BY
CYNTHIA GILLOOLY

94

wildflowers

Plaids, hayrides, and marshmallows melting on sticks—ah, the memories that autumn wildflowers call to mind! Although there are many elements in this carefree design, it's easy to make if you take your time and follow the step-by-step instructions. Once you complete this project, you'll never again be intimidated by designs with lots of flowers.

what you need

Stylish metal basket

Dried green sheet moss, 2 blueberry fall foliage stems, 2 burgundy fall foliage stems, 1 blackberry fall foliage stem, 4 orange fall berry stems, 3 milkweed raceme stems, 3 yellow yarrow stems, 2 fall wild grape stems each with 4 grape clusters, 2 brick-colored grape clusters, 2 brick-colored berry clusters, 8 burgundy cosmos, 1 red freesia, and 1 rust hydrangea

Instant deluxe floral foam for fresh flowers, serrated knife, sticky floral foam tape, floral wire or U-pins, and floral tape as needed

what you do

1. The instant deluxe floral foam is made to use with large fresh flowers. But used dry, it provides a sturdier base than regular foam for silk plants which have many heavy pieces. With the serrated knife, cut the foam to fit snugly into the basket. To insure the foam stays securely in the basket, tape it to the edges of the basket with the sticky floral foam tape. Use the tape to make a diagonal "X" over the foam, pull the tape taut, and stretch it about an inch (2.5 cm) over the edge of the basket.

2. Pull the dry moss slightly to loosen the fibers so that you can insert the flower stems through it. Cover the foam with the moss.

3. Insert the more linear foliage, such as the blueberry and fall foliage stems, into the foam to establish the scale and shape of the arrangement. Then insert the berry spikes, such as the burgundy and brick-colored berries. Leave the center of the arrangement lower than the two ends to create a crescent shape.

4. Add the larger fall foliage—the wild grape stems—to the edge of the container to soften the line and create a look of spilling-over abundance.

5. Begin adding flowers, such as the cosmos, in groupings to create the feeling of flowers growing naturally in a field.

6. Create a center of interest with the grape clusters. Make a hairpin of floral wire or use U-pins to hold the grapes in place. Draw attention to the focal point by adding other berry clusters to draw the eye to the lower, darker center of the arrangement.

96

DESIGN BY
CATHY BARNHARDT

7. Continue filling out the arrangement with the remaining foliage and flowers, drawing the eye to the grapes. Be sure to vary the length of the stems and bend them to add to the look of wildflowers growing naturally. Again, cluster the flowers such as the bright yellow yarrow and the milkweed racemes to give a very natural feeling to the design.

8. Place the red freesia and the rust hydrangea on opposite sides of the front center section, to continue to draw the eye to the center.

9. Complete the design by adding a few more berry spikes and wild grape clusters to add interest and abundance.

design tips

Meadow designs such as this one are easy to make for each season of the year. All you do is substitute flowers, branches, and berries appropriate to the particular season. Choose containers that also reflect the mood and color palette of that time of year. Enjoy experimenting!

orchid window box

Delicate. Stunning. Easy. Easy? Yes! One of the joys of working with silk flowers is the fact that some of the most awe-inspiring arrangements are so easy to make that even a beginner can accomplish them successfully. The trick is to plan your design carefully and remember that in Japanese-style arrangements such as this one, a subtle touch is a powerful one.

what you need

Metal and wooden window box

Spanish and green moss, 1 phaelanopsis orchid stem with foliage, 3 lavender dendrobium orchids stems, 2 orchid foliage stems, strappy green latex foliage, 1 silk oncidium stem, curly willow branches, and lichen or some other natural accent

Serrated knife, floral foam, and scissors

what you do

1. Use the serrated knife to cut the floral foam to fit snugly into the window box.

2. Cover the foam with the two mosses.

3. Place the phaelanopsis orchid into the center of the container, manipulating the stem so it looks realistic. (Use the photo to guide you.)

4. Place one of the lavender dendrobium stems on the right. Add the second stem lower than the first one, also to the right. Place the last dendrobium so that it's low in the design, flowing out toward the front from the lip of the container.
    This creates a sense of depth in the design.

5. Insert orchid foliage behind the dendrobium flowers.

6. Insert the strappy green leaves on the left side of the container.

7. Place the oncidium orchid so it emerges from the center of the strappy foliage. Again, manipulate the stem so it imitates the natural growth habit.

8. Place a few branches of the curly willow gracefully behind the orchids and the leaves.

9. Place the lichen or other natural accent in the back to add depth to the arrangement.

design tips

This arrangement is so beautifully done that you can learn a handful of design lessons just by imitating it. Notice the delicate balance between shape and space, between color and greenery, and how the entire arrangement rises up magnificently from the simple flat wooden box. Orchids are terrific plants for one-minute home decorators because unlike other plants, such as daffodils and lilacs that are thought of as season-specific, orchids are considered perfect all year long. Branch out, literally, by trying a design made only with branches and berries, or one with grasses of different shapes and colors. Whatever combination of plant materials you try, remember to utilize space as one of your key design elements.

DESIGN BY
CNTHIA GILLOOLY

reflections of ranunculus

Double the loveliness of any flower by placing several specimens in a shiny, reflective vase. For even more impact, display the arrangement in front of a mirror. Create height by artfully arranging the foliage.

what you need

Reflective container

6 or more ranunculus, some with buds, and foliage to match

Scissors or wire cutters

what you do

1. With the scissors, cut off the leaves at the bottom of the stem and set them aside.

2. Cut the flower stems and arrange them in the container. This arrangement can be designed to stand flat against a wall, as in the photograph. If you want to make an in-the-round design (for which this arrangement is perfect), increase the number of flowers. Notice the use of buds—they always add a nice touch of variety to a design.

3. Insert the leaves you cut off in step 1 into the arrangement to rise proudly above the flowers and balance them with the size of the vase.

design tips

Any flower truly looks awesome in a vase with a reflective surface. Consider silver, aluminum, and mirrored finishes. Remember to balance the number of flowers and their heights and shapes with the container and the foliage you use.

DESIGN BY
SUSAN McBRIDE

blooming boxes

Small paper and balsa wood boxes bloom with colorful flowers. Children love making these pretty projects, so get their help making extra boxes for last-minute surprise gifts. For a personalized touch, make paper gift cards and tie them on with shiny cord.

what you need

Gift boxes in varying shapes and sizes (found in craft stores)

Silk flowers and foliage of your choice

Raffia, ribbon or twine, scissors, floral wire, wire cutters, floral tape, craft paint, paintbrush, awl (optional), adhesive tape, felt or fabric, hot-glue gun and glue sticks

102

what you do
round box

1. Paint the bottom section of the box in the color of your choice. Let it dry completely.

2. With the awl or tip of a sharp scissors, punch a few holes (depending on the size of the box) into the lid. (Kids love to punch holes in things, so stay with them to make sure they don't get carried away!)

3. Remove the leaves from the flower stems. Depending on the size of the box lid and the flowers, trim the flower stems to a length about 1½ inches (3.8 cm). Make bundles of three or five flowers and poke them through the holes. Fill the holes until the lid is no longer visible underneath. Bend the stems back flat against the inside of the lid and tape or hot glue them securely.

4. Cut a circle of pretty fabric or felt that matches the color of your flowers and hot glue it to the inside of the lid to hide the tips of the stems.

5. Hot glue the leaves around the outer edge of the lid, hiding about half of each leaf in the flower mound.

what you
rectangular box

1. Crisscross three strands of raffia around the center of the box, tie into a tight knot, and cut off the ends.

2. Make a small, tight arrangement of little flowers and foliage. Cut the stems to an even length of 2 inches (5 cm). Wrap the stems in the wire; then wrap with the floral tape.

3. Cut 10 pieces of raffia, each about 10 inches (25.4 cm) long. Tie a bow with all the pieces around the stems of the small bouquet. Trim off the ends in varying lengths. With one or two pieces of raffia, tie the bouquet and bow onto the crisscrossed raffia, and trim the ends.

what you do
small square box

1. Paint the box in the color of choice. Let it dry completely.

2. With the awl or tip of the scissors, punch a hole in the center of the lid.

3. Place a single flower with greenery into the hole. Tape the stem flat back against the inside of the lid and tape it securely. Cover the inside of the lid with fabric to hide the taped flower and hot glue it in place.

103

design tips

Once you've decorated a few balsa wood boxes, try working with more luxurious boxes, such as glittery paper boxes. Rescue vintage jewelry boxes—which are often undamaged inside—by covering their outsides with silk flowers.

DESIGN BY

SUSAN McBRIDE

mondo burgundy

When light strikes black mondo grass, it reveals its fascinating range of colors, from ebony to deep wine-burgundy. Dramatic, easy to make, and absolutely no upkeep—no wonder everyone loves this design.

what you need

Sturdy planter

4 bunches black/burgundy mondo grass

Serrated knife, floral foam, black pebbles, hot-glue gun and glue sticks

what you do

1. With the serrated knife, cut the floral foam so that it fits snugly into the planter. Leave about 3 inches (7.6 cm) of space from the top of the planter to the foam.

2. Apply hot glue glue around the bottom sections of the mondo grass stems to reinforce them in case you decide to put the arrangement outside where it may be blown by the wind. Insert the stems into the floral foam until they are secure.

3. Arrange the upper blades of mondo grass to create a full and balanced spray of grass.

4. After the glue has set, place the pebbles around the base of the grass, making sure that they fully cover the foam.

design tips

Make an attention-getting display that consists of several heavy pots with grasses of different colors and heights. Match the color of the pebbles to each grass and container. For a more edgy look, use crystal chips, sea glass, or porcelain shards instead of the pebbles.

DESIGN BY

TOM METCALF

wintry centerpiece

Combine the traditional holiday colors of green, red, and white in an unconventional way that is both festive and supremely elegant. For a bigger holiday splash, use small red and pink poinsettias instead of the ranunculus, or go bold with big crimson gerbera.

what you need

Shallow rectangular container

Green Spanish moss, 5 cedar stems, 4 blue juniper stems, 3 variegated juniper stems, ½ bush of variegated red, white and green winter ivy, 4 holly stems with berries, 3 double stems of white freesia (total of 6 blooms), 3 red ranunculus stems, 3 white waxflower stems, and 2 princess rose stems

Serrated knife, floral foam, floral tape, floral picks, and wired wooden picks

what you do

1. With the serrated knife, cut the block of floral foam to fit into your container. With the floral tape, secure the foam to the container. Cover the foam with the Spanish moss and hold it in place with the floral picks.

2. Insert one long stem of cedar on each end. Cut the other cedar stems to length to create an oval shape and insert them all around the foam. For example, the shape for this design measured 36 x 18 x 10 inches (91 x 45.7 x 25.4 cm).

3. In between the cedar stems, add the two types of junipers, the winter ivy, and the holly, blending in the variation of color and shape in the leaves.

4. Now for the flowers. Add the freesias first. Leave two of the freesia stems long and insert them on either end of the arrangement. Cut the other freesia stems to the length you need to blend in with the evergreens. Then add the ranunculus, the waxflowers, and the princess roses. Keep the flowers spaced at a graceful distance from one another, so each one can be noticed. Use the wired wooden picks if needed. If there are buds, be sure to insert them, too, for they add subtle variety.

design tips

To make a similar arrangement for autumn, keep the greenery and use flowers such as chrysanthemums, marigolds, cone daisies, and lavender. For spring, use tulips, paper whites, and some dwarf iris.

If you'd like to use a small pillar candle in the center of the arrangement—it would look marvelous—cut the shape of the candle into the foam and place the candle before you start.

DESIGN BY

SUSAN PARTAIN

tabletop topiary

The wild tangle of berries at the base contradicts the manicured green globes at the top, giving the whole topiary a mischievous look. Once you learn how easy it is to make one tabletop topiary, you'll probably want to make a whole forest.

what you need

Sturdy container, with a heavy or weighted base, tall and wide enough to hold the topiary

6 stalks of winter berries in shades of red, some with leaves, others without, and moss

Serrated knife, floral foam, hot-glue gun and glue sticks, wire cutters, and a prefabricated topiary with 2 balls on a stick (found in craft stores)

what you do

1. With the serrated knife, cut the floral foam and fit it into the container.

2. Trim some of the moss and cover the foam, using the hot glue.

3. With the wire cutters, trim the stalks of red berries and their foliage to lengths of 4 to 5 inches (10.2 to 12.7 cm).

4. Insert the berry stalks into the foam around the edge of the container. Gently bend them to cascade downward over the edge. The effect should be a bit of a tangle, a natural-looking mass of color and round red shapes. Spread out the green leaves to add some height.

5. Insert the topiary stick into the center of the berry patch. Shore it up with a bead of hot glue if necessary, so it stands up perfectly straight.

6. Place the topiary on a table, mantle or display shelf. Make many of them and use them as centerpieces for party tables.

design tip

Make your own "green" topiaries by glueing layers of moss or evergreens onto polystyrene shapes such as balls or cones. Once the moss coverage is complete, pierce the shape with a straight stick or dowel to create a stand. Decorate the bottom of the topiary any way you like, using berries, fruits, flowers, or foliage. Make fantastic flower topiaries merely by inserting a stick into flower-covered pomanders and placing them in appropriate containers. Se the *Sassy Pomanders* project on page 92.

108

DESIGN BY
SUSAN MCBRIDE

mounded roses

Once you realize that short is just as beautiful as tall, making arrangements for wide-mouthed vases can be remarkably easy. All you need is one type of flower—in this case big, delicately shaded roses—to shape them into a low, fulsome mound. The result is gracious and classy.

what you need

Low, wide container

8 or more delicately shaded big roses

Serrated knife, floral foam, and scissors

what you do

1. Cut the floral foam to fit snugly into the vase, just below the rim.

2. Remove most of the leaves from the rose stems and cut the stems to fit into the vase. Insert the roses into the foam so they form a pleasing mound around the rim of the vase.

3. Let some of the top leaves peak out tentatively from the roses to add just a touch of green.

4. Place the arrangement in a space where its low, sturdy design is a benefit, such as on your bedside table where it won't get knocked over when you reach out to shut off the alarm clock.

design tips

For other simple mound arrangements, use camellias, small sunflowers, dahlias, or lisianthus. Once you've learned the mound technique, try something more risky: a two-tiered arrangement. Place a tall central cylinder of flowers (wrapped in ribbon perhaps, such as the *Daffodil Tree with Gemstones* project on page 46) and surround it with a circle of mounded flowers. Lovely!

110

DESIGN BY

SUSAN MCBRIDE

bride's bouquet

For the most important bouquet in a woman's life, give it the once-in-a-lifetime attention it deserves. The detailed care taken for each stem creates a luxurious, hand-tied look. One romantic advantage of a bride's bouquet made of silk flowers is that it can remain forever as beautiful as it was on the day she carried it down the aisle.

what you need

3 stems of cream spray roses, 1 bloom of creamy white roses (with 3 open blooms, 2 buds, and 3 tight buds), 4 full lavender stems (cut into pieces), pieces of cream and green variegated ivy

3 yards of wired satin ribbon, pearl corsage pins, floral wires, wire cutters, scissors, and light moss-green floral tape

what you do

1. Wire and tape each flower and foliage stem with two or three wraps of the floral tape. (Remember to pull the tape first.) Yes, this takes time, but it gives you more control of the placement and shaping of the bouquet. Cut the stems to lengths of 8 to 10 inches (20.3 to 25.4 cm). Add a wire stem to give length to any shorter pieces (see page 000 for instructions). Save the extra foliage.

2. Place the larger roses together to create a focal point, slightly varying their heights. Use creamy white rather than stark white roses. The softer shades and variations add interest. To create a more natural look, use flowers of varying sizes and stages of development, such as tight buds, partially opened buds, and fully opened blooms.

3. Add the smaller clusters of spray roses around and between the larger roses. As you are adding flowers, remember to slightly bend the wire stems out from the bouquet center, and stagger the heights of the flowers slightly to create the look of a mound of flowers. Don't place the flowers too close together—space is an important part of design.

4. Add some of the lavender filler flowers as you work, wherever you feel the design needs the color or interest.

5. Add small pieces of ivy to accent the center roses.

6. Go back and place more of the lavender to concentrate the color and accent a rose or add depth. Cut the pieces to varying lengths, bend them slightly, use tips or fuller pieces for interest and naturalness.

7. Finish off the underside of the bouquet with the extra rose foliage taken from discarded stems. Wrap the taped wire stems with the ribbon, using the corsage pins to hold the ribbon in place.

8. Add a bow for the finishing touch.

DESIGN BY

CATHY BARNHARDT

caketop posy

A posy is a small bouquet given for sentimental reasons. Make the happy couple's day even more unforgettable with a caketop posy designed especially for them. Without words it says, "Love Always."

what you need

7 creamy white spray roses with buds, 3 stems of viburnum, 3 stems of sweetpeas with buds, 5 stems of freesia with buds, 2 stems of lavender (cut into 6 pieces) and variegated ivy leaves

Floral wire, wire cutters, scissors, and light moss-green floral tape

what you do

1. Know the diameter of the caketop so you can plan the size of your posy, or bouquet, accordingly. As you can see from the photograph, we made a small posy that covered the top of a modest-size cake.

2. Tape and wire each piece in the same manner as the Bride's Bouquet on page 112, creating small wired stems that can be shaped. Snip each individual flower and add an ivy leaf, then wire and tape it. Give the posy some graceful, lighter pieces such as the lavender and viburnum, to add height and naturalness to the design. Use little bits and pieces, not too much of one thing or another, and especially show the different flower buds. Use the photograph to guide you.

4. Use the foliage snipped from stems to finish off the bottom of the posy. The foliage makes a nice background for the flowers and contrasts with the cake icing, which sets off the posy's design.

5. After all of the materials have been placed and secured, use the wire cutters to trim off the stems, staggering their lengths to create a point.

6. Use the floral tape to wrap all of the stems together and make a waxed pointed base. Push the posy into the caketop and press it in so it's secure.

114

DESIGN BY
CATHY BARNHARDT

wedding vase

With this exquisite arrangement, you'll symbolize your wishes to the new couple:
"May marriage join the two of you forever in the vessel of Life. May it overflow with
luxury, beauty, harmony, and balance."

what you need

Blue and white porcelain vase

**5 spirea, 4 green hydrangea, 3 balloon
flowers, 2 blue echnops bushes with globes
and foliage (or thistles), 6 freesia stems
with 3 flowers each, 2 white rose stems
with 3 blooms each, 2 yellow rose stems
with 3 blooms each, 2 spray roses, 8 sweetpeas, and 36 stems of lavender**

**Marbles, floral wires, wire cutters, scissors,
and light moss-green floral tape**

what you do

1. Arrangements in tall vases can be
top heavy, so stabilize the vase with
glass marbles in the bottom.

2. Make a stem-grid to help hold
the other stems in place as you
arrange them.
• Crisscross the spirea stems inside
the vase, establishing the width of
the arrangement.
• Crisscross the two larger
hydrangea stems from front to back,
near the rim. This will also establish
the depth of the design.

• Crisscross two of the balloon flowers, from opposite sides. You have
now created a grid of six stem-Xs to
help hold the other stems in place as
you arrange them.

3. Establish the height of the
arrangement by inserting the
remaining three spirea twigs—the
marbles and the stem-grid you created will hold them in place. You'll
basically be weaving the stems
together in the vase as you work.

4. Place the two echnops bushes on
opposite sides of the arrangement.
Their many stems will also help to
keep the rest of the materials in
place.

5. Place the remaining large, bold
flowers—the two hydrangeas and
the balloon flower—near the center
sections.

6. Cut the different roses from the
main stem, being sure to show the
different stages of development
(bud, partially open blossom, and
full blossom) and insert them. Cut
flowers off the main stem to create
an open feeling where needed and
to fill in other sections.

7. Add the more delicate flowers,
the freesia and sweet peas. Finally,
add the stems of lavender as filler
and color accent.

116

DESIGN BY
CATHY BARNHARDT

arranging silk flowers for the wedding

With an event as important as a wedding, it's essential to have a harmonious relationship among all the flower arrangements. In the photo are three key elements in a typical wedding ensemble: the bride's bouquet, the caketop posy, and the wedding vase, projects from pages 112 to 117. Let's not forget the bridesmaids' bouquets, the men's boutonnières, the women's corsages, the tabletop centerpieces, the wreaths, the garlands—whew! A happily-flowered wedding means lots of planning. Here are some tips to guide you.

dear bride-to-be,

Unless you're an expert floral designer with lots of time, don't make your own arrangements. Wedding flowers *always* take more time than you expect. Bestow the job on someone who is doing nothing else for your wedding but your flowers, a trusted friend with proven silk flower experience.

dear wedding silk flower designer,

Meet with the bride well in advance of the wedding date to discuss all her needs. Work with color swatches of the wedding colors to select flower colors. When designing your displays, remember to reflect the season in which the wedding takes place and the time of day, as well as the wedding style (formal or informal). Be sure to include flowers that have personal significance for the new couple.

Make a list of all the desired arrangements: for the bride, the bridal party, the wedding itself, and the reception afterwards. See the instructions for other projects in the book and modify them as you desire, such as the wreath (page 60), the swag (page 88), the pomanders (page 92), and the centerpiece (page 106).

Visit the site of the wedding so you know your arrangements will be suitable to the surroundings.

Keep to the budget, with both the bride's money and your time.

Always keep extra supplies on hand. Have helpers to assist you in transporting the flowers and displaying them in plenty of time.

Since the bride will want to keep her bouquet, it would be a lovely idea to make another one just like it and set it aside. When it comes time to throw the bouquet, she can toss the duplicate.

Coordinate the bridesmaids' bouquets with the colors of their dresses, and differentiate them from the bride's bouquet by using other ribbon colors.

design tips

You can easily modify the ingredients listed on page 116 for the wedding vase project. Keep the roses, since they are the most traditional flowers in wedding arrangements, and make substitutions for the other flowers. Here are a few suggestions:

To make a boutonnière, snip an individual flower, add a leaf of ivy, and wrap it all tightly with floral tape. Use a corsage pin to attach it securely to the lapel. Make corsages for mothers and other special women in the same way—just add more flowers and leaves. Coordinate the corsages with the wedding colors but don't make them so elaborate that they take attention away from the bride's bouquet.

Have fun at the wedding! The joy of silk flowers is that you can arrange them for everyone at the wedding to enjoy—and then you don't have to fuss with them for another minute.

- White spray orchids instead of spirea
- Small peonies instead of hydrangeas
- Cornflowers instead of balloon flowers
- Bachelor buttons instead of echinops
- Stephanotis or tuberose instead of freesia
- Russian sage instead of lavender
- Heather or stock or sweet William instead of sweetpeas

sending flower messages

We all know that a dozen red roses usually means someone is trying to say the words "I love you." But most of us are unaware that there are many different languages, or codes of meaning, that have been given to flowers over the ages.

Any single flower or combination can have many different meanings. Some flower meanings are ancient, coming from prehistoric myths and various spiritual traditions. Some are endearingly old-fashioned, such as the complicated language of flowers developed by the Victorians to send secret love messages. Others are simple, such as the flowers associated with astrological signs or connected to specific months in the same way as birthstones are.

Not every flower has a meaning already assigned to it by tradition. Many of us make up our own meanings for the flower gifts we give, feeling inspired by the flower itself on the spur of the moment. Sometimes that inspiration touches the poet in each of us, making our accompanying words as important as the flowers. At other times, words fail us, and the flowers themselves express what we cannot.

Here are some examples of the many different messages that your silk flower gifts can give. Have fun making your own translations!

Of course you send Mom flowers on Mother's Day, and usually roses, which are the universal symbol of love. But wouldn't she be thrilled with gifts from her far-flung children that said "Happy Mother's Day!" every day of the year? That's what displays of silk roses do— they're as fresh-looking after months on the dining room table as they were the day they were delivered. Give Mom a different arrangement each year and she can display reminders of her children's thoughtfulness in every room in the house.

What *does* a man want? Trying to figure out what kinds of silk flowers to give a man can be bewildering. Here's a sure-fire solution: don't give him flowers— give him non-flowers. Arrangements with simple grasses and spare Ikebana-influenced projects are so unfussy that (even if they won't admit it) men really do love to receive them as gifts.

Making flower arrangements that relate to travel can be just as much fun as the trip itself. The Sunny Tuscany arrangement is a perfect welcome home gift for travelers who left their hearts in Italy. Consider flip-flopping the travel idea— how about an English cottage garden silk flower arrangement as an encouraging push to your friend who has always wanted to see the gardens of Kent?

The chrysanthemum, one of the noble flowers in Chinese symbology, is also the flower for those born in November. Because chrysanthemums withstand the cold, they represents enduring friendship—and become thoughtful gifts any time of year for a friend who is going through a difficult time or grieving the loss of a loved one.

To the Chinese, the magnificent peony represents longevity and prosperity, so these flowers make wonderful good-luck messages that relate to business and finance. They're ideal for students starting their first big job, or as congratulations on a career promotion. Peonies would be an excellent choice to display in the lobby of an attorney or financial advisor. It sends out an unmistakable message: "You'll be prosperous if you bring your business to us!"

Small arrangements that hang on walls are fantastic presents for people who don't have much space for vase displays. Wouldn't a smaller version of the Sylvan Wall Sconce look marvelous on the wall near your computer screen? As you work, the display reminds you "Creativity is everywhere." Imagine a bigger version for someone moving into their first apartment—the pretty sconce relieves the loneliness of empty walls and says "Welcome Home" as soon as it's put up.

Sunflowers, being the quintessential summer flower, make incredibly good off-season arrangements for those folks who need a pick-me-up during the winter. The sunflower is also the birth flower for Leos, and those playful lions of the zodiac love to be surrounded with their signature flowers. (There's no such thing as a single sunflower for a Leo—they always have to have a bunch!) Silk sunflowers also make terrific party displays. No matter what time of year it is, the sunflowers shout "Let's party!""

Hand-made presents openly proclaim their message: "This gift is for you. Made with love." You can personalize any gift by adding silk flowers that have meaning for the recipient, such as for their birth or zodiac sign, which is an especially fun thing for children to do. Here's a list of birth month flowers:

January ....Carnation
February...Violet
March ....Daffodil
April ....Daisy
May ....Lily of the Valley
June..Rose
July ....Delphinium
August ....Gladiolus
September ....Aster
October ....Marigold
November......................Chrysanthemum
December...Holly

121

selecting
silk flowers: checklist

Before you select the silk flowers and other elements you need for your arrangement, use this checklist to help you focus your decisions. Feel free to copy this checklist and take it with you when you buy flowers from a floral or craft supply store.

122

1. What is the reason I want to make this particular arrangement?
   - ○ cheer up a dark corner
   - ○ impress visitors when they walk in the door
   - ○ give as a present
   - ○ decorate for a celebration or holiday
   - ○ change an arrangement to match the current season of the year
   - ○ want something new

2. What style should it have?
   - ○ traditional
   - ○ country
   - ○ contemporary
   - ○ ultra-modern
   - ○ Ikebana-inspired
   - ○ whimsical
   - ○ whatever inspires me when I see it
   - ○ something totally unexpected

3. Where will the arrangement be?
   - ○ living room
   - ○ hallway
   - ○ family room
   - ○ kitchen/dining room
   - ○ master bedroom
   - ○ baby's or child's room(s)
   - ○ bathroom(s)
   - ○ guest room
   - ○ workshop
   - ○ home office
   - ○ outdoor patio or porch or in the garden
   - ○ office or workspace

4. In which area of the room do I want the arrangement displayed?
   - ○ on or against a wall
   - ○ on a pedestal
   - ○ on a low table
   - ○ on a bedside table
   - ○ on a dining table
   - ○ on or in a bookcase or entertainment center

○ on a kitchen countertop

○ on a bathroom shelf
or commode top

○ in an unlit fireplace or on
the mantel

○ in the reception area or
meeting room at work

○ next to my computer screen

5. What arrangement size and
shape best fits that area?

○ short ○ tall

○ horizontal ○ vertical

○ front-facing ○ all-around

○ symmetrical ○ asymmetrical

○ round ○ triangular

○ rectangular ○ oval

○ centerpiece for table that
is _____ long

○ wreath in the shape of

_____

6. What colors in the room do
I want to highlight? Which ones do
I want to de-emphasize? (Bring paint
strips or fabric swatches or your color
wheel with you.)

7. What kind of container do I
have already for the arrangement?
(Take it with you to the store to
experiment with what flowers look
best in it.) If I need a new container,
how will it coordinate in color, shape,
size, and texture with the location I
have planned for it?

8. Which flower(s) will be
the focal flowers? Line flowers?
Filler flowers? Do I need additional
foliage?

9. What accessories, such as
artificial bugs or butterflies, would
enhance the display?

10. What tools may I need that I
don't already have? Are there any
supplies, such as foam and floral
tape that I need to replenish?

contributing designers

124

Roger Ballew is a Visual Merchandiser at the Biltmore Estate. He shows off his eclectic and natural style in his favorite projects—large-scale natural arrangements with sticks and vines. He lives happily in Asheville, North Carolina, with his dog and two cats.

Cathy Barnhardt has been the chief floral designer at Biltmore House in Asheville, North Carolina, America's largest privately owned home and historic landmark, for 25 years. She enjoys creating large-scale, dramatic pieces as well as more natural "gathered" designs for events and homes. In addition to her free-lance floral design home-based business, she's a frequent designer for magazines and other Lark books. cathybarnhardt@aol.com. (828) 684-0139

Muriel Edens owns Moon Creek Flowers, providing wildflowers, heirloom flowers, organic vegetables and culinary herbs to local markets in the Asheville, North Carolina area. She also designs flowers for weddings, special events, and fine restaurants.

Cynthia Gillooly spent 23 years as a floral designer with shops in Sanibel Island, Florida, and Asheville, North Carolina. She currently owns and operates Saracena Design, an interior plantscape business that allows her to indulge her passion for growing orchids. (828) 776-9010

Beth Hohensee began her floral career in 1982 in New York when she opened her own shop. Today she is the head designer/manager of Flower Gallery, in Asheville, North Carolina. Beth is passionate about flowers, her family, and life on the farm in Waynesville, North Carolina.

Susan McBride is a graphic designer and multi-media artist, who also loves gardens and animals. She designed floral arrangements for weddings and special events in Atlanta, Georgia. Susan, her husband, daughter, and pets live in Asheville, North Carolina.

Luck McElreath is the owner/designer of Flower Gallery, located in Asheville, North Carolina, which opened in 1982. Luck enjoys travel and international cuisine. She is the adoring grandmother to four grandsons. She lives in Weaverville, North Carolina. flowergalleryluck@earthlink.net. (828) 258-8427

Tom Metcalf is an art director with Lark Books, responsible for making eight beautiful books a year. In his spare time he's an avid gardener and floral designer, specializing in Ikebana-inspired designs.

Susan Partain has been a member of the floral display staff of the Biltmore Estate for six years. She loves any creative work with flowers, especially projects in the English country garden style. She has three children and one grandson. She and her husband live in Candler, North Carolina.

Kenneth Trumbauer is the Retail Events Manager for the Biltmore Estate in Asheville, North Carolina. In addition to frequent contributions to Lark Books and private design consultations for clients, Kenneth has worked for various retailers, including Saks Fifth Avenue, Pier One Imports, and Neiman Marcus. He lives in Asheville, North Carolina.

Marcianne Miller is the author of several Lark Books, including *Decorating with Mini-Lights* (2002), *The Ultimate Gel Candle Book* (2002), and *Salvage Style for the Garden* (2003). She came to book writing via previous careers in broadcasting and archaeology. She and her family live in Asheville, North Carolina, with lots of pets and many ever-changing displays of silk flowers.

125

Thank you to all who made this book possible...

art director Susan McBride, who blessed
every page with her Celtic charm and
the elegance of an Empress

photographer Keith Wright, who kissed every
flower with light (www. keithwright.com)

Our Lark Books team:
publishing director Carol Taylor
senior editor Deborah Morgenthal
cover designer Barbara Zaretsky
assistant art director Hannes Charen
production assistant Shannon Yokeley
art intern Lorelei Buckley
administrative assistant Delores Gosnell

proofreader Diane Weinstein
technical consultant Caroline Jaynes-Winslow

Victoria Baynes at The Golden Cricket
in Asheville, North Carolina,
for her contribution of materials

Elizabeth Bennett Cauley
and Edna M. Kahl
for the contribution
of their vintage containers

index